THE GOOD MANAGER'S GUIDE

77 practical checklists for day-to-day management

TREVOR BOUTALL

Request for Comment

We would like to know what you think of this guide and how you are using it. We are particularly interested to know of any way in which its content, language, style or layout could be improved so that it would better meet your needs.

Please send your comments to: MCI, Russell Square House, 10-12 Russell Square, London WC1B 5BZ.

Acknowledgements

Thanks to Tim Kidd, Joe McCullagh, Penny Foxton, Karen Marshall, Beryl Nelms, Jill Sinclair, Mike Stringfellow for contributing to the text and production of this guide.

Thanks also to the thousands of managers particularly those from Auto Windscreens, Burnley Healthcare NHS Trust, Kwik Save Stores, London Electricity, Magistrates Courts' Service, National Westminster Bank, RNIB and Woolwich Building Society who tested drafts of the checklists.

Copyright

Published by the Management Charter Initiative, the operating arm of the National Forum for Management Education and Development, Russell Square House, 10-12 Russell Square, London WC1B 5BZ. Registered Charity No. 1002554.

The Good Manager's Guide 1995
ISBN 1 897587 20 1

Contents

How to use this guide

The manager's role is complex. Managers are often required to perform a number of functions simultaneously, drawing on a wide repertoire of skills and a broad suite of technical and specialist knowledge as well as common sense. They are required to respond to fast-changing circumstances and work at many different levels.

To many managers, the job of management remains a mystery, a journey in a foreign land full of the terrors of the unknown. This guide seeks to chart that territory and to show that, although the problem may be complex, the answer is often simple.

The *Good Manager's Guide* breaks the management role down into simple, practical checklists to help you tackle everyday tasks successfully. There is no magic in it, just crystal clear objectives and strictly logical steps.

The checklists can be used for a variety of purposes, such as job descriptions, recruitment, appraisal schemes and performance management. However, they are designed, first and foremost, to help you do your job. Here are some examples of how you might use them.

Addressing unfamiliar tasks

You may be faced with a task you have not performed for a long time, or perhaps never met before. Take recruiting a new member of staff for example. How would you go about it?

The contents page tells you that, under *Managing People*, there is a section on *Personnel Planning*. There are three checklists to help you. *Planning human resource requirements* will help you check whether recruitment is the

> **Contents**
> ▶ Managing People
> ▶ Personnel Planning
> ▶ 3 checklists

best option at this stage. *Drawing up job specifications* will help you clarify what the job entails and the sort of person who would be suitable. *Assessing and selecting staff* will give you guidance on how to choose the right person for the job.

Tackling important tasks

You may have to do something critically important which you want to ensure you get right - running an important meeting for instance.

The keywords index at the back of the book points you to the checklist for *Leading meetings*. This will help to ensure you get the best from all participants, arrive at

> **Keywords Index**
> ▶ Meetings
> ▶ Leading
>   ▶ Leading meetings

well-informed decisions and get there in the fastest possible time.

Checking that you are doing things properly

Preparing budgets for your plans and projects may be something you do on a regular basis but you may like to check occasionally that you are doing things properly.

The contents page shows there is a section on budgets under *Managing Finance*, with a checklist specifically for *Preparing budgets*. There are also

> **Contents**
> ▶ Managing Finance
> ▶ Managing Budgets
>   ▶ Preparing budgets

useful checklists to help you negotiate, agree and monitor your budgets.

Carrying out a public task

Some aspects of management are more public than others, so it is important not just to get it right, but to be seen to get it right.

For example, *Defining your organisation's mission* involves consultation and discussion with all your stakeholders, and needs careful negotiation to ensure it attracts the widest possible support.

You should find checklists to cover all your management tasks, though they may not cover all your specialist functions. They are based on the national Management Standards, developed by the Management Charter Initiative (MCI). If you can prove that

> **Keywords Index**
> ▶ Mission
> ▶ Defining
>   ▶ Defining your
>   organisation's
>   mission

you are competent in all the areas covered by these checklists, you could qualify for a National Vocational Qualification or Scottish Vocational Qualification in Management. Refer to pages 143-154.

Operational Management

What is Operational Management?

The key purpose of management is to achieve the organisation's objectives and continuously improve its performance.

Operational management is being clear about the objectives you have to achieve through your team, in your department or for your part of the business; and using the available resources to best effect.

It involves managing the operation of your part of the organisation as effectively as possible; being clear about what you are expected to deliver; designing systems and procedures; and organising the workplace to achieve this. Always you need to be looking for, and implementing, ways of doing things better to provide a quality service or product every time.

Operational management means getting things done through people. You have to make sure you have the right people to do the job. You have to develop a team and help each member of the team develop the skills they need to perform their job effectively. You need to plan the work and allocate it amongst the team, setting individual objectives and providing feedback on their performance. Managing people involves building effective working relationships and dealing with difficult problems, being careful to be fair and equitable in all your dealings.

As a manager, you will often be required to prepare budgets for the expenditure, and perhaps income, for your part of the operation. It is your responsibility to ensure that these financial targets are met and that all staff are aware of how they can help in improving the financial performance. Operational management also involves obtaining and using information to aid decision-making; and leading and participating effectively in meetings to arrive at decisions.

Operational Management

Managing the Operation	Managing People
Meeting Customer Needs	Personnel Planning
Managing Change	Developing Teams and Individuals
Quality Assurance	Managing Teams and Individuals
Time Management	Working Relationships
	Managing Problems with Staff
	Equal Opportunities

Managing Finance	Managing Information
Managing Budgets	Using Information
Cost Control	Meetings

Operational management is a complex business requiring a range of skills and knowledge, together with disciplined time-management, if you are to succeed. However, the checklists in this book provide some simple, practical guidelines for effectively tackling everyday tasks. You will find them relevant whether you are a team leader, supervisor or manager at any level, although you may find your role is to contribute to, rather than have full responsibility for, an activity.

Managing the Operation

Managing the Operation is about working out ways of meeting customer requirements on time, every time. It involves:

Meeting Customer Needs   **13**

Establishing and agreeing customer requirements   14
Maintaining supplies   15
Maintaining a productive work environment   16
Meeting customer specifications   17
Solving problems for customers   18

Managing Change   **19**

Identifying opportunities for improvements   20
Assessing the pros and cons of change   21
Negotiating and agreeing the introduction of change   22
Implementing and evaluating changes   23

Quality Assurance   **25**

Assuring quality   26

Time Management   **27**

Managing your time   28

Meeting Customer Needs

This section is about maintaining an effective operation to meet customer needs.

The checklists will help you to:

- be clear about the needs of your customers
- ensure suppliers provide value for money
- maintain a safe and efficient working environment
- design your operational systems to meet customer specifications
- solve problems for customers when things go wrong.

The process of *Meeting Customer Needs* looks like this:

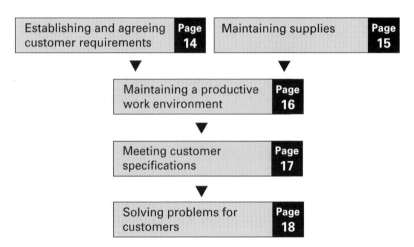

Establishing and agreeing customer requirements	Page 14
Maintaining supplies	Page 15
Maintaining a productive work environment	Page 16
Meeting customer specifications	Page 17
Solving problems for customers	Page 18

Meeting Customer Needs

Establishing and agreeing customer requirements

1. **Research your customers' needs** - use formal and informal techniques to identify the services or products your customers, or potential customers, need.

2. **Design your services or products to meet your customers' needs** - and ensure your services and products meet legal and organisational requirements and resource constraints.

3. **Describe your services or products clearly** - explain your services or products to customers, think about the person you are talking to, and make sure you communicate in a manner and at a pace which is appropriate.

4. **Encourage customers to discuss their requirements** - invite them to seek clarification wherever appropriate and tell you how well you are meeting their needs.

5. **Communicate frequently with customers** - develop a relationship of trust and goodwill, and keep them informed about any changes which affect them.

6. **Ensure agreements meet legal and organisational requirements** - consult specialists if you are in doubt.

7. **Negotiate effectively** - use your experience of past negotiations to ensure the success of future negotiations.

8. **Optimise agreements** - create a 'win-win' situation, where you achieve your objectives whilst meeting customer needs.

9. **Draw up detailed specifications** - ensure that specifications of customised services or products contain all the relevant information to allow customer requirements to be met.

10. **Keep accurate records** - include all relevant information about customer agreements and implementation plans.

11. **Design customer-focused operations** - organise your operations to provide the most efficient service to your customers.

12. **Develop helpful staff** - encourage your staff to put the customers first and to take personal responsibility for meeting customer needs.

Meeting Customer Needs

Maintaining supplies

1. **Identify the supplies you need** - check they are sufficient to meet customer requirements.

2. **Identify and develop suitable sources of supply** - make sure your suppliers can provide you with the materials you need for your product and services; always have alternative suppliers available for contingencies, if possible.

3. **Select suppliers objectively** - apply fair criteria in choosing your suppliers.

4. **Review your suppliers regularly** - check they continue to offer best value for money and quality of service.

5. **Keep accurate records of suppliers and supplies** - keep a complete list of suppliers' details and monitor levels of supplies regularly.

6. **Watch market and economic trends which may affect supplies** - keep an eye on factors such as raw materials cost/availability, competitor activity or changes to legislation which may affect the price or availability of supplies.

7. **Take action where there are likely to be problems or opportunities with supplies** - where your information suggests changes to supplies which may give you problems or opportunities, take, or recommend, appropriate action to turn the situation to your advantage.

8. **Keep complete and accurate records of negotiations and agreements with suppliers** - and pass this information on to appropriate people as soon as possible.

9. **Maintain goodwill** - throughout your negotiations with suppliers, make sure you retain their goodwill, and find mutually acceptable ways of settling any disputes.

Maintaining a productive work environment

1. **Ensure the environment is as conducive to work as possible** - involve your staff in assessing the work environment to see if there are different ways it could be arranged to improve productivity.

2. **Ensure that conditions satisfy legal and organisational requirements** - check the relevant legislation and your internal guidelines, and make sure you have a safe work environment.

3. **Cater for special needs** - provide for any special needs of employees or potential employees to ensure they can work productively.

4. **Make sure equipment is properly maintained and used only by competent personnel** - regularly check all equipment in your area to see that it is properly maintained and that relevant staff have been trained to use it.

5. **Ensure you have a sufficient supply of resources** - plan what materials, equipment and resources you require to keep your operation running smoothly.

6. **Where you do not have sufficient resources, refer to the appropriate people** - let them know immediately if you are likely to run out of anything.

7. **Pass on recommendations for improving conditions** - where you identify opportunities for improving working conditions, let the appropriate people know right away, so the organisation can benefit as soon as possible.

8. **Report accidents and incidents promptly and accurately** - check that you, and your staff, are fully aware of the accident and hazard procedures and that they are followed at all times.

9. **Keep accurate records** - make sure your department's maintenance and health and safety records are accurate, legible and up-to-date.

Meeting customer specifications

1. **Check that specifications are clear, complete and accurate** - where there is any omission or ambiguity, get clarification from your customer.

2. **Draw up plans and schedules to meet these specifications** - allow for contingencies in these plans.

3. **Brief all relevant people** - make sure they understand how the specifications, plans and schedules affect them.

4. **Monitor operations** - monitor what is happening and take appropriate action to ensure specifications are met.

5. **Make best use of resources** - use your human, capital and financial resources efficiently to meet the specifications.

6. **Encourage staff to take responsibility for meeting customer requirements** - involve staff in finding the best way to meet specifications and gain their commitment.

7. **Give staff feedback** - tell them how well they are doing in meeting customer requirements.

8. **Get feedback from customers** - use this feedback to improve future operations.

9. **Minimise disruptions to operations** - take appropriate action to reduce any factors which may disrupt operations.

10. **Take corrective action** - implement any changes without delay and inform relevant staff, colleagues and customers about these.

11. **Monitor corrective action** - make sure that changes are working, and use this experience to improve future operations.

12. **Keep complete and accurate records of operations** - keep records of activities and how well you met customer specifications and make these records available to appropriate people.

Meeting Customer Needs

Solving problems for customers

1. **Design systems to anticipate and avoid problems for customers** - design all your procedures to meet customer needs.

2. **Advise customers about your policies and procedures for solving their problems** - use appropriate media to publish your policies and procedures and alternative sources of assistance to which customers may refer.

3. **Identify and acknowledge the customer's perception of the problem** - where problems do occur, listen carefully in order to understand and acknowledge the customer's view of the problem.

4. **Gather all information relevant to the customer's problem** - refer to records and other people involved in order to get a full picture of the problem.

5. **Summarise the customer's problem** - summarise their perceptions and all other relevant information and check that the customer agrees with your summary of the problem.

6. **Keep the customer informed** - tell the customer how you plan to resolve the problem, how long it will take and give the customer progress reports where appropriate.

7. **Refer to organisational procedures** - examine and interpret procedures for handling customer complaints to identify a solution.

8. **Seek advice from colleagues or senior managers** - where organisational procedures do not offer a satisfactory solution ask colleagues for help in identifying alternative solutions.

9. **Implement the solution promptly** - once the solution has been identified, take prompt action to solve the customer's problem and inform the customer of the action taken.

10. **Monitor the delivery of the solution** - and make appropriate modifications to resolve any problems arising.

11. **Check customer's satisfaction** - where appropriate, check that the problem has been solved to the customer's satisfaction.

12. **Develop new procedures** - review the process and where policies or procedures do not offer a satisfactory solution, revise or develop new policies or procedures to avoid or address similar situations.

Managing Change

This section is about identifying, implementing and evaluating improvements.

The checklists will help you to:

- always be looking for areas where improvements can be made
- assess the benefits against any problems caused by the changes
- consult with all concerned to get them to agree to the changes
- implement your plans for change
- evaluate whether improvements have been achieved.

The process of *Managing Change* looks like this:

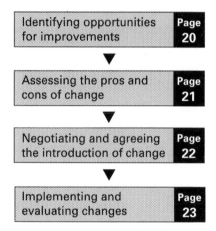

Identifying opportunities for improvements

1. **Keep up to date with developments in your sector** - make sure you get relevant, valid, reliable information from various sources on developments in materials, equipment, technology and processes.

2. **Consider the importance of these developments to your organisation** - carry out a regular review of developments and analyse their significance to your organisation.

3. **Pass information on developments to the appropriate people** - if you think it is important, make sure your colleagues, staff and senior managers are aware of its significance.

4. **Identify opportunities for improvements** - use information on developments to identify opportunities for growth, improvements in procedures or improvements in quality.

5. **Monitor and evaluate your operations continuously** - always look for areas where improvements can be made and take appropriate action.

6. **Identify any obstacles to change** - take appropriate measures to alleviate any problems which may prevent improvements being made.

7. **Learn from your experience** - use your experience of previous improvements to help identify new ones.

Assessing the pros and cons of change

1. **Get complete and accurate information** - make sure you have
    sufficient, reliable information on both current and proposed
    services, products and systems to allow you to make a reliable
    assessment.

2. **Compare the advantages and disadvantages** - use qualitative and
    quantitative techniques to assess the pros and cons of current and
    proposed services, products and systems.

3. **Assess the implications of introducing changes** - changes may
    affect cashflow, working practices, staff morale, supply and
    distribution networks and customer loyalty; anticipate and assess
    the likely effect of changes.

4. **Take into account previous assessments of introducing change**
    - look at how realistic previous assessments turned out to be and
    use these to modify your current assessment.

5. **Present your recommendations to the appropriate people** -
    make your recommendations to senior managers or specialists in a
    way which helps them make a decision and in time to allow the
    decision to be put into effect.

6. **Amend your recommendations in the light of responses** - make
    appropriate alterations to your recommendations on the basis of
    the responses you get from senior managers and specialists.

Negotiating and agreeing the introduction of change

1. **Present information on projected change to the appropriate people** - let staff, colleagues, senior managers and others know about the changes at the earliest possible time, and in sufficient detail, to allow them to evaluate its impact on their area of responsibility.

2. **Conduct negotiations in a spirit of goodwill** - make sure you retain the support of others and find mutually acceptable ways of settling any disputes.

3. **Make compromises where appropriate** - it may be necessary to make compromises to accommodate other priorities, but make sure these compromises are consistent with your organisation's strategy, objectives and practices.

4. **Reach an agreement in line with your organisation's strategy** - and include detailed implementation plans.

5. **Keep records of negotiations and agreements** - make sure your records are complete and accurate and that they are available for others to refer to if necessary.

6. **Where you could not secure the changes you anticipated, tell your staff in a positive manner** - sometimes you are disappointed in not being able to obtain the changes you wanted for your team due to other organisational priorities; explain to your staff the reasons for this in a positive way.

7. **Encourage all relevant people to understand and participate in the changes** - communicate the changes and their effects to people, and gain their support.

Implementing and evaluating changes

1. **Present details of implementation plans to all concerned** - make sure that you brief everyone involved, or affected by, the changes on their role in the changes and the possible impact on their area.

2. **Encourage people to seek clarification** - check on their understanding of their role and encourage them to ask questions.

3. **Use resources in the most effective way** - plan carefully so that you meet the new requirements as cost-effectively as possible.

4. **Monitor the changes** - check to see that the changes have been implemented according to plan and that they result in the improvements anticipated.

5. **Evaluate the benefits of the changes** - compare the new way of working with the old; are the benefits as expected?

6. **Modify implementation plans and activities in the light of experience** - you may need to modify the way you implement changes to cope with unforeseen problems.

7. **Review the change process** - review the whole process of identifying, assessing, negotiating, agreeing, implementing and evaluating change, note ways of doing it better next time and make appropriate recommendations to senior managers, colleagues and specialists.

Quality Assurance

This section is about developing systems to ensure that you meet your customers needs on time, every time.

The checklist will help you to:

• be clear about your customers' needs

• involve staff and other colleagues in developing quality assurance systems

• monitor and publicise the benefits of quality assurance systems.

This section links closely with the sections on *Meeting Customer Needs* and *Managing Change.* It has just one checklist:

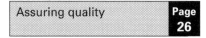

| Assuring quality | Page 26 |

Quality Assurance

Assuring quality

1. **Be clear about your customers' expectations and requirements** - quality is about fulfilling your customers' expectations on time, every time.

2. **Make recommendations for quality assurance systems to meet customers' expectations** - make sure your systems are in place to meet customer requirements, not to satisfy a bureaucratic whim.

3. **Encourage staff to help develop quality assurance systems** - consult the staff who are most involved with the operation to get their ideas and gain their commitment to following the quality assurance system.

4. **Present details of the quality assurance system, or modifications to it, to all those concerned** - make sure that you brief everyone involved or affected by the quality assurance system on their role or the possible impact on their area.

5. **Encourage people to seek clarification** - check on their understanding of their role and encourage them to ask questions.

6. **Make the best use of resources** - make sure your quality assurance system does not duplicate or add unnecessarily to the workload, but makes best use of existing procedures and activities.

7. **Publicise the benefits and results of quality assurance** - enhance employee commitment and customer satisfaction by making sure they are aware of the benefits that the quality assurance system is delivering.

8. **Monitor your quality assurance systems** - check whether they continue to deliver customer satisfaction and make any modifications required.

Time Management

This section is about making the most efficient use of your time.

The checklist will help you to:

- be clear about your objectives and your priorities
- plan your time and allow for contingencies
- delegate work where appropriate
- be decisive.

This section will help you with all other aspects of management. It has just one checklist:

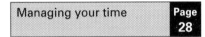

| Managing your time | Page 28 |

Managing your time

1. **Be clear about your objectives** - be clear about what you have to achieve, by when and what the priorities are.

2. **Identify what needs to be done to achieve these objectives** - identify what you, and others, need to do to achieve your objectives and estimate how long each activity will take.

3. **Plan your time** - plan these activities into your time on an annual, monthly, weekly and daily basis to ensure objectives are achieved on time; include time for evaluation.

4. **Delegate** - review your activities and, where possible, delegate those activities which could be done equally well by one of your staff, with training and guidance where appropriate.

5. **Handle paper once only** - when dealing with paper, decide immediately to respond, refer, file or destroy.

6. **Take decisions** - when faced with a choice, either make your choice or decide what further information you need to be able to make an informed choice.

7. **Control interruptions** - make it clear when you welcome consultation with others, and when you require uninterrupted time to complete an activity.

8. **Control digressions** - keep your objectives in mind and do not indulge in, or allow others to indulge in, digressions.

9. **Allow for contingencies** - allow time in your planning for additional activities or for activities to overrun.

10. **Review your activities** - review your progress towards your objectives on a regular basis and reschedule activities as necessary.

Managing People

Management is about meeting customer requirements with and through people. It involves:

Personnel Planning

This section is about making sure you have the right people to do the jobs.

The checklists will help you to:

• be clear about the people you need to meet your organisational objectives

• specify the skills, qualities and attributes you are looking for in staff

• assess candidates against specific criteria and select those most appropriate

• make redundant those staff who are no longer required.

The process for *Personnel Planning* looks like this

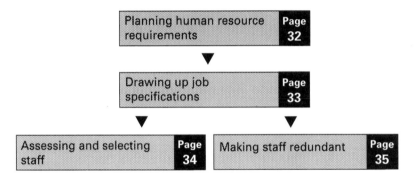

Planning human resource requirements

1. **Identify the optimum human resources required to achieve objectives** - you will need people to help you achieve the objectives of your organisation, department, team or project; identify the number and type of staff needed to provide you with the best support at the most reasonable cost.

2. **Base your plans on current, valid and reliable information** - check your information is sound and up-to-date.

3. **Support your plans with appropriate calculations** - your estimates of the human resource required will need to be supported by calculations of the time required to complete tasks and the associated personnel costs, including training and development, and provision for special needs.

4. **Identify the skills and personal qualities required of the team and individuals** - look for a balance of strengths within the team.

5. **Be clear about organisational constraints** - specify where financial considerations, organisational policy or legal constraints affect your plans.

6. **Consult with colleagues and staff** - take into account the views of your colleagues, specialists and your staff on how best to meet your future human resource requirements.

7. **Present your plans on time and with the appropriate level of detail** - make sure your plans are accurate, contain sufficient detail for a decision to be made and are presented in time for you to take the necessary action.

Drawing up job specifications

1. **Be clear about the job role** - clearly state the purpose of the job and how it relates to organisational objectives and the team.

2. **Specify the job in sufficient detail** - think carefully about the job title, reporting relationships, key objectives and responsibilities and the terms and conditions of service.

3. **Specify the type of person required** - be clear about the knowledge, competences and qualities they will need.

4. **Consult with colleagues and staff** - take into account the views of your colleagues, specialists and your staff on the definition of the job and the skills, knowledge and qualities required.

5. **Check that the specification is clear, concise and complies with legal and organisational requirements** - consult with specialists if you are in doubt.

6. **Agree the specification with appropriate people** - check and agree the specification with colleagues, specialists and your staff before taking any action to recruit, transfer or change a person's job.

7. **Regularly review job specifications** - keep specifications under review to ensure that they still describe the job and meet the organisation's needs.

Assessing and selecting staff

1. **Check your organisation's procedures and legal requirements** - make sure that your process for assessing and selecting staff complies with your organisation's procedures and the law.

2. **Obtain, or draw up, criteria against which to judge candidates** - have clear, measurable criteria.

3. **Seek advice if you are not sure about any of the selection criteria** - consult with specialists if you are in doubt.

4. **Get sufficient information from candidates to be able to make a decision** - use a variety of appropriate assessment techniques, cv's, application forms, interviews, tests, references etc, to ensure you get all relevant information.

5. **Judge the information obtained against specified selection criteria** - you should be able to defend your decision to accept or reject a candidate by how well the candidates meet the selection criteria; do not let irrelevant factors affect your decision.

6. **Be fair and consistent** - correct any deviations from agreed procedures before you make your selection.

7. **Maintain confidentiality** - tell only authorised people of your selection recommendations.

8. **Keep clear, accurate and complete records** - you may need to refer back to them.

9. **Keep candidates informed** - tell candidates promptly and accurately of decisions following each stage of the selection process.

10. **Check that your choice is justifiable** - make sure you have selected the most suitable candidate from the evidence obtained and the process used; if in doubt, consult colleagues or specialists.

11. **Review the process and make appropriate recommendations for improvement** - consider every aspect of the process and make any recommendations for improving it, so that you and your colleagues can do better next time.

Personnel Planning

Making staff redundant

1. **Keep staff informed about current procedures** - ensure that staff are aware of your organisation's policy and any redundancy procedures, including appeals procedure.

2. **Avoid redundancies where possible** - accurate personnel planning will minimise the need for redundancies, but where these are inevitable explore alternatives such as early retirement or part-time working.

3. **Consult with staff** - consult with both individual staff and their representatives over the redundancy plan. Consultation will improve co-operation and may result in alternative, more acceptable approaches being adopted.

4. **Agree clear and fair selection criteria** - agree selection criteria which are unambiguous, can be clearly applied, are fair and comply with legal and organisational requirements.

5. **Apply selection criteria fairly and consistently** - consult with specialists if you are in doubt.

6. **Prepare to break the news** - rehearse what you will say to staff who will be made redundant, including responses to likely questions, and enlist the support of colleagues or specialists, as advised.

7. **Break the news quickly and compassionately** - tell staff quickly, clearly, confidentially and compassionately that they will be made redundant and what help is available to them.

8. **Offer alternative work** - where there are suitable jobs available, offer these alternatives with details of terms and conditions.

9. **Offer counselling** - offer staff appropriate counselling, resources, training and time off work to help them find another job and cope with the personal and practical implications of redundancy.

10. **Seek advice** - seek advice from colleagues and specialists, on all aspects of making staff redundant in order to ensure you comply with legal and organisational requirements.

11. **Keep staff and colleagues informed** - tell staff and colleagues about the redundancies and the reasons, without breaching confidentiality.

12. **Recommend any changes to policy or procedures** - tell the appropriate people of ways in which your organisation's policy or procedures could be improved.

Developing Teams and Individuals

This section is about making sure your team has the skills to do their jobs.

The checklists will help you to:
- develop a balanced team with all the skills needed
- help individuals identify and develop the skills they need
- develop the skills you need for your job
- coach individuals to develop new skills
- be an adviser or mentor to individuals to help them develop
- evaluate and improve the training and development processes.

The process for *Developing Teams and Individuals* looks like this:

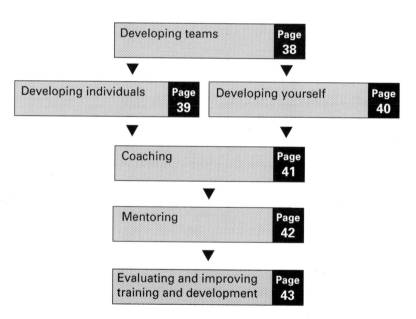

Developing teams

1. **Involve all team members in evaluating the team's development needs** - get them involved in identifying their own strengths and weaknesses.

2. **Assess the team's strengths and weaknesses** - looking at each individual and at the team as a whole, assess and acknowledge the team's strengths and weaknesses to carry out current and future work.

3. **Consult with all team members on how to meet development needs** - gain the team's commitment by involving them in planning how to meet development needs.

4. **Be clear about the objectives of development plans** - your objectives should be clear, relevant and realistic for individuals and the team as a whole.

5. **Optimise the use of resources** - when planning development activities, use available resources effectively.

6. **Minimise unproductive friction** - be clear about individuals' responsibilities in the team to minimise risk of bad feeling.

7. **Regularly review your plans** - discuss and agree improvements to development plans with team members, other colleagues and specialists at appropriate intervals.

Developing Teams and Individuals

Developing individuals

1. **Involve individuals in identifying their own development needs** - get them to identify their own strengths and weaknesses.

2. **Discuss development needs and plans with individuals** - gain their commitment by involving individuals in planning how to meet their development needs.

3. **Be clear about the objectives of development plans** - your objectives should be clear, relevant and realistic for the individual.

4. **Balance business needs with individual aspirations** - plans should help individuals to develop the skills they need to do their current job and meet future job requirements and career aspirations.

5. **Optimise the use of resources** - when planning development activities, use available resources effectively.

6. **Regularly review your plans** - regularly discuss and agree improvements to development plans with individuals, other colleagues and specialists.

Managing People

Developing yourself

1. **Take responsibility for developing yourself** - ensure you develop the skills you need to achieve your objectives.

2. **Identify your own strengths and weaknesses** - measure your current skills as a manager against appropriate standards and by getting feedback from your line manager, colleagues and staff.

3. **Set yourself clear development objectives** - make your objectives achievable, realistic and challenging.

4. **Consider the needs of the organisation** - include objectives to develop as a team member.

5. **Allow sufficient time and resources** - allocate sufficient time and appropriate resources to achieve your development objectives.

6. **Regularly review progress and performance** - check your progress against your objectives with your line manager and specialists at regular intervals and revise your plan as appropriate.

7. **Compare feedback with your own perceptions of your performance** - compare feedback from your line manager, colleagues, staff and others with how well you think you are doing; and improve your future performance as a result.

Coaching

1. **Identify the individual's development needs** - use appropriate methods to assess the needs of the person you are coaching.

2. **Agree learning objectives** - discuss and agree with the individual the learning objectives to be achieved.

3. **Take account of the individual** - design your coaching to match the individual's learning preferences, and deliver the coaching in a manner and at a pace appropriate to the learner.

4. **Analyse the components of skills** - make sure you understand the different components of the skill and convey these in the sequence in which they need to be learnt.

5. **Identify inhibiting factors** - clearly identify and discuss with learners any factors which are inhibiting their learning.

6. **Check learners' progress** - check regularly on progress and modify coaching as appropriate.

7. **Give feedback** - provide timely feedback to learners on the process of learning and on their progress towards learning objectives in a positive and encouraging manner.

8. **Receive feedback** - ask learners how they feel about the process of learning and their speed of progress and modify coaching as appropriate.

Mentoring

1. **Identify the individual's learning objectives** - discuss and identify the learning objectives to be achieved with individual mentees, their line managers and others involved.

2. **Agree the support mentees require** - specify and agree the roles, responsibilities and resources needed to help mentees achieve their learning objectives.

3. **Identify and overcome any difficulties in obtaining this support** - identify likely difficulties in obtaining the necessary · people and resources and agree ways of overcoming these difficulties.

4. **Develop effective working relationships** - both with mentees and with others who can provide support.

5. **Provide guidance** - provide accurate, timely and appropriate advice and guidance on learning methods and opportunities, and on other sources of information and advice.

6. **Encourage independent decision-making** - provide guidance in a way which encourages mentees to take responsibility for their own development and enables them to make informed decisions.

7. **Facilitate learning and assessment opportunities** - identify and facilitate opportunities for mentees to develop, practice, apply and assess new skills, knowledge and experience in a structured way.

8. **Provide on-going support** - within the agreed role, provide mentees with support for their learning, development and assessment, as required.

9. **Give feedback** - provide timely feedback to mentees on their progress towards learning objectives in a positive and encouraging manner.

10. **Review the mentoring process** - at appropriate intervals, discuss the mentoring process and your relationship with mentees and modify as appropriate.

Evaluating and improving training and development

1. **Identify clearly the training and development objectives** - be clear what the objectives are and how to measure whether they have been achieved.

2. **Debrief the learners** - discuss with individuals and teams involved in training and development how useful it was, how satisfied they were with its delivery and how well it will apply to their work.

3. **Find suitable alternatives where training and development did not meet the needs** - discuss and agree with the individuals and teams concerned alternative training and development which may be more appropriate.

4. **Modify team and individual training and development plans** - where plans were unrealistic, discuss and agree modified plans with the teams and individuals concerned.

5. **Check whether objectives have been achieved** - apply the agreed measures to see to what extent objectives have been achieved.

6. **Pass on your experience** - discuss the strengths and weaknesses of the training and development processes used with specialists, your line manager and colleagues so they can gain from your experience.

7. **Benefit from your experience** - use your experience of training and development processes to help you identify more appropriate training and development in the future.

Managing Teams and Individuals

This section is about making sure your team get the job done.

The checklists will help you to:

- plan the work to meet your objectives
- allocate work amongst the team
- set clear objectives for each member of the team
- evaluate performance and provide feedback to staff.

The process for *Managing Teams and Individuals* looks like this:

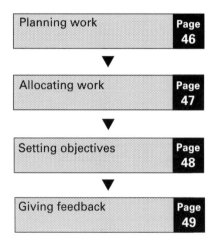

Managing People

Planning work

1. **Plan work in order to meet organisational objectives** - make sure your plans are consistent with team and organisational objectives.

2. **Assess the degree of direction required by each member of staff** - inexperienced or less confident staff may need far more direction and help in planning their work than more experienced and self-assured colleagues.

3. **Encourage individuals to contribute to planning work activities and methods** - the staff who will be carrying out the work are likely to have sound ideas as to the most efficient ways of doing it.

4. **Include staff suggestions on working methods, resources and time required** - this will help to ensure their commitment to the work.

5. **Select work methods and activities which meet both operational and developmental objectives** - choose work methods and activities which balance management priorities, organisational objectives, legal requirements and opportunities for individual development.

6. **Select cost-effective work methods** - choose work methods which make the best use of available material, capital and people.

7. **Seek advice where legal requirements and organisational/ developmental objectives conflict** - consult with your line manager, specialists or external advisers.

Allocating work

1. **Allocate work according to availability of resources and skills of staff** - optimise the resources and the skills of the staff available to meet organisational objectives.

2. **Clearly define team and individual responsibilities and limits of authority** - make sure staff understand their own responsibilities and limits of authority, and those with whom they work closely, in order to avoid possible conflict, duplication or omission of important responsibilities.

3. **Provide learning and developmental opportunities for staff within the work allocated** - take opportunities to develop new skills which staff will need in the future.

4. **Brief staff on their work in a manner and at a level and pace which is appropriate** - inexperienced or less confident staff may need a more detailed briefing on their responsibilities and work than their more experienced and self-assured colleagues.

5. **Encourage staff to seek clarification** - check on their understanding and give them opportunities to ask questions.

6. **Provide access to people who can help them meet their objectives** - staff may need access to colleagues, managers, specialists and external advisers to help them meet their work and developmental objectives.

7. **Provide the right level of supervision** - some staff will require much closer supervision than others.

8. **Ensure that work allocations are realistic** - carefully calculate the time, cost and criticality of the work to ensure appropriate resources have been allocated.

9. **Reallocate work where appropriate** - if the way work was allocated proves to be unrealistic, or organisational demands change, reallocate work whilst minimising any detrimental impact on time or cost.

10. **Benefit from your experience** - evaluate how well you have allocated work in order to improve your performance in the future.

Setting objectives

1. **Involve staff in setting objectives** - ask staff to be proactive in identifying what their objectives should be.
2. **Set clear objectives** - agree SMART objectives with your staff which are:

Specific	- be precise about what must be achieved
Measurable	- how will you know if it has been achieved?
Agreed	- by you, the member of staff and the team
Realistic	- objectives have to be achievable
Time-bound	- to be completed by a specified time.

3. **Explain objectives clearly** - when explaining objectives, think about the person you are talking to, and make sure you communicate with them in a manner and at a pace which is appropriate.
4. **Encourage staff to seek clarification** - check on their understanding and give them opportunities to ask questions.
5. **Update objectives regularly** - review objectives as often as appropriate in the light of changes to individual and team workloads and organisational priorities.
6. **Check that objectives have been achieved** - as part of the objective-setting process, agree the date when you will review with your staff whether the objectives have been achieved.
7. **Provide feedback** - both formally and informally which includes constructive suggestions and encouragement for improving future performance.

Giving feedback

1. **Seek opportunities to provide feedback to teams and individuals on their performance** - feedback helps people to understand if they are doing a good job or if there are areas in which they can improve. Feedback can be given formally or informally, orally or in writing.

2. **Choose an appropriate time and place to give the feedback** - feedback is more useful and relevant if provided quickly. Sometimes it is appropriate to give feedback publicly, but often a quiet word with a member of staff is what is required.

3. **Recognise good performance and achievement** - take opportunities to congratulate staff on their successes.

4. **Provide constructive suggestions and encouragement for improving future performance** - when staff are not performing well, tell them, and advise them how they can improve.

5. **Encourage staff to contribute to their own assessment** - ask open-ended questions about how they view their performance and invite them to be specific.

6. **Provide feedback in sufficient detail and in a manner and at a level and pace which is appropriate to the staff concerned** - some staff may readily understand your feedback on their performance, with others it may be necessary to be very specific about their performance and any improvements required.

7. **Encourage staff to seek clarification** - check their understanding and give them the opportunity to ask questions.

8. **Encourage staff to make suggestions on how systems/ procedures could be improved** - their performance may be greatly enhanced by changes to procedures and working practices.

9. **Record details of any action agreed** - make a note of actions agreed to maintain or improve their performance or change procedures, and inform the appropriate people.

10. **Review performance** - check back at an appropriate point to see whether performance has improved or been maintained.

Working Relationships

This section is about building effective working relationships with all those you work with.

The checklists will help you to:

- take time to build effective working relationships
- consult with colleagues and keep them informed
- be honest and open with people
- provide support and keep your promises
- take steps to minimise any possible conflicts.

The process of building effective *Working Relationships* looks like this

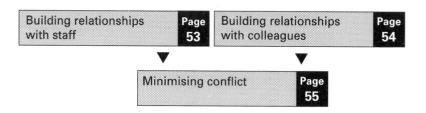

Building a relationship with your manager

1. **Keep your manager informed** - provide an appropriate level of detail about activities, progress, results and achievements.

2. **Provide information about emerging threats and opportunities** - let your manager know about possible threats and opportunities clearly, accurately and with the appropriate level of urgency.

3. **Seek information and advice** - ask your manager for information and advice on policy and ways of working whenever appropriate.

4. **Present clear proposals for action** - present proposals at the appropriate time and with the right level of detail. Your manager will require more detail the greater the degree of change, expenditure and risk involved in your proposal.

5. **Identify the reasons why a proposal has been rejected** - try to find out clearly what the reasons are and, if appropriate, put forward alternative proposals.

6. **Make efforts to maintain a good relationship with your manager** - even if you do have disagreements, try to prevent these damaging your relationship.

7. **Meet your objectives** - always try to fulfil the objectives agreed with your manager in full; where circumstances prevent you from meeting objectives, inform your manager at the earliest possible time.

8. **Support your manager** - give your manager your backing, especially in situations which involve people outside your team.

9. **Be open and direct** - discuss any concerns about the relationship with your manager directly with him or her.

Building relationships with staff

1. **Take time to build honest and constructive relationships with staff** - get to know your staff and allow them to get to know you.

2. **Keep staff informed** - provide them with relevant information on organisational policy and strategy, progress, emerging threats and opportunities.

3. **Consult staff about proposed activities** - give them the opportunity to state their views so they can be taken into account.

4. **Encourage staff to offer their ideas and views** - use open questions to get their contributions.

5. **Give recognition for their ideas and views** - thank them and show the value you place on their ideas.

6. **Give clear reasons where ideas are not taken up** - where it is not possible to take up a good idea, acknowledge the value of the idea and explain why it is not possible to adopt it.

7. **Encourage staff to seek clarification** - check their understanding and give them the opportunity to ask questions.

8. **Keep your promises** - when you make promises and undertakings to staff, make sure they are realistic and that you honour them.

9. **Support your staff** - give staff your backing especially in situations which involve people outside your team.

10. **Be open and direct** - discuss concerns about the quality of work directly with the member of staff concerned.

Building relationships with colleagues

1. **Take time to build honest and constructive relationships with colleagues** - get to know your colleagues and allow them to get to know you.

2. **Encourage open, honest and friendly behaviour** - ask open questions to get their opinions.

3. **Share information and opinions with colleagues** - stop and think who could benefit from any information or idea you have.

4. **Offer help and advice with sensitivity** - you can often help a colleague or provide advice on a difficult problem.

5. **Deal courteously with colleagues when you have differences of opinion** - you will not always agree with colleagues; discuss these different views respectfully and try to understand them.

6. **Resolve conflicts amicably** - always maintain mutual respect.

7. **Keep your promises** - when you make promises to colleagues, make sure they are realistic and that you honour them.

Working Relationships

Minimising conflict

1. **Explain to staff the standards of work and behaviour you expect** - some staff will readily appreciate the standards you and your organisation require; others may require a fuller and more detailed explanation.

2. **Clearly allocate work and responsibilities** - you can greatly reduce the potential for conflict by making sure your staff are clear about the responsibilities of each member of the team.

3. **Encourage staff to discuss problems which affect their work** - make it clear that you are available to help resolve these problems.

4. **Quickly identify potential or actual conflicts between staff** - when conflicts appear, or are likely, involve the relevant staff in identifying the nature and cause of the conflict early on.

5. **Take prompt action to resolve conflicts** - do not let the conflict fester, but take decisive action to deal with it.

6. **Ensure solutions satisfy legal and organisational requirements** - check that you are not infringing any legislation or procedures and that your solution helps meet organisational objectives.

7. **Keep accurate and complete records of the conflict** - particularly where the conflict is serious, keep notes of what happened and what was agreed, in case there is any comeback.

8. **Monitor the situation** - keep an eye on the situation to ensure that the conflict does not reappear.

9. **Learn from your experience** - use the experience to help you, and your staff, avoid or quickly resolve conflicts in the future.

Managing Problems with Staff

This section is about ensuring the best outcome when you have problems with staff.

The checklists will help you to:

- counsel staff when personal matters are affecting their work
- action grievance and disciplinary procedures
- dismiss staff, where this is the most appropriate option.

This section covers:

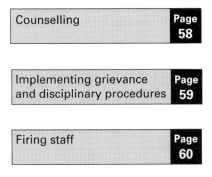

| Counselling | Page 58 |

| Implementing grievance and disciplinary procedures | Page 59 |

| Firing staff | Page 60 |

Managing Problems with Staff

Counselling

1. **Identify the need for counselling quickly** - be alert to the need to counsel staff; changes in mood, a fall-off in performance, stress symptoms, or a word from a colleague may indicate the need to counsel staff.

2. **Choose an appropriate time and place** - counselling on personal matters affecting an individual's work needs to take place in a private place and at a time which allows for full discussion without interruptions.

3. **Follow your organisation's guidelines or personnel policies** - if your organisation has specified personnel policies, check to make sure you follow these.

4. **Encourage the individual to discuss the situation fully** - help the individual to understand the situation and all the factors which affect it.

5. **Encourage the individual to take responsibility for their own decisions and actions** - remember you are helping them to solve a problem, you are not solving it for them.

6. **Recommend an appropriate counselling service where appropriate** - when you do not have the skills or knowledge to help the individual, recommend they see a specialist in your organisation or an external counselling service, doctor etc.

7. **Monitor the situation** - keep an eye on the situation and offer further counselling sessions if these are necessary.

Implementing grievance and disciplinary procedures

1. **Keep staff informed about current procedures** - make sure they have up-to-date copies of your organisation's grievance and disciplinary procedures and remind them of these from time to time.

2. **Action grievance and disciplinary procedures with minimum delay** - act promptly to prevent the situation getting out of hand and causing damage to the organisation or the staff concerned.

3. **Act in accordance with legal and organisational requirements** - check, with a specialist if necessary, both the legal situation and your organisation's procedures.

4. **Ask for advice** - where appropriate, confidentially ask a specialist, your line manager or colleagues for advice on how to deal effectively with these difficult situations, especially where legal and organisational requirements conflict.

5. **Involve a third party** - where appropriate, ask a third party - specialist, line manager or colleague - to become involved to ensure you implement the procedures fairly and impartially.

6. **Be, and be seen to be, impartial** - get all the facts of the case before you and make decisions which are objective and can be shown to be free of personal bias.

7. **Keep accurate and complete records** - make detailed notes of the whole proceedings and, where appropriate, copy these to the member(s) of staff concerned and specialists.

8. **Monitor the situation** - keep an eye on the situation to ensure that the problems which led to the implementation of grievance or disciplinary procedures do not reappear.

9. **Learn from your experience** - use the experience to help you, and your staff, avoid or quickly resolve the problems in the future.

10. **Recommend any improvements to the procedures** - tell the appropriate people of any ways in which the procedures could be improved.

Firing staff

1. **Avoid the need to fire staff wherever possible** - good recruitment and selection, training, development and counselling techniques will minimise the need to fire staff.

2. **Follow disciplinary procedures** - make sure you follow your organisation's disciplinary procedures in detail.

3. **Seek advice** - seek advice from colleagues and specialists, inside or outside your organisation, on all aspects of firing staff in order to ensure you comply with legal and organisational requirements.

4. **Involve a third party** - where appropriate, ask a third party - specialist, line manager or colleague - to become involved to ensure you follow procedures fairly and impartially.

5. **Get the facts** - make sure you get all information relevant to the dismissal. If necessary, suspend the member of staff on full pay until you have all the facts available.

6. **Prepare to break the news** - rehearse what you will say to the member of staff, including responses to likely questions, and enlist the support of colleagues or specialists as appropriate.

7. **Give clear, fair grounds for dismissal** - check that your reasons for dismissing the member of staff are clear and fair grounds for dismissal, and give these both orally and in writing.

8. **Summarily dismiss staff in the case of gross misconduct** - dismiss staff without notice or pay in lieu of notice in the event of gross misconduct. When in doubt, suspend on full pay until you can consult specialists or gather all the facts.

9. **Keep staff and colleagues informed** - tell staff and colleagues about the dismissal and the reasons, without breaching confidentiality.

10. **Review the procedures and reasons for dismissal** - tell the appropriate people of any ways in which the procedures could be improved or future dismissals avoided.

Equal Opportunities

This section is about providing equal working opportunities, encouraging diversity and discouraging unfair discrimination.

The checklists will help you to:

- develop, implement and evaluate your equal opportunities policy and action plan
- encourage staff to use a range of appropriate working styles
- promote fair working practices.

The process of managing *Equal Opportunities* looks like this:

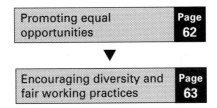

Promoting equal opportunities	Page 62

▼

Encouraging diversity and fair working practices	Page 63

Managing People

Promoting equal opportunities

1. **Contribute to the development of your organisation's equal opportunities policy** - offer your views and recommendations on how the policy should be developed.

2. **Involve staff, colleagues and customers** - encourage them to help develop your equal opportunities action plan, identify areas where opportunities are unfairly restricted and gain their commitment to the plan.

3. **Agree measures** - specify the criteria by which you can assess progress in your action plan.

4. **Collect and analyse information** - find out whether some groups of potential customers are excluded from obtaining your services or products; check whether certain employees, or potential employees, are denied access to development, employment or promotion opportunities.

5. **Identify the strengths of all employees** - especially those from under-represented groups, and identify how these strengths can contribute to your organisation's objectives.

6. **Identify special needs** - identify any special needs of customers, potential customers, employees or potential employees.

7. **Publish your action plan** - including actions to meet special needs and address any imbalances, as well as taking positive action to support under-represented groups.

8. **Communicate action plan to staff** - make sure staff are aware of their responsibilities and duties within the equal opportunities policy and action plan.

9. **Provide training and development opportunities** - provide appropriate training and development to help staff fulfil their duties in the action plan.

10. **Implement your action plan and evaluate your performance** - use agreed measures to monitor your progress against the action plan and modify the plan as appropriate.

Equal Opportunities

Encouraging diversity and fair working practices

1. **Communicate your equal opportunities policy to staff** - make sure staff are aware of the standards of behaviour expected of them and the consequences of unacceptable behaviour.

2. **Encourage a diversity of working styles** - encourage staff to develop a repertoire of appropriate working styles.

3. **Support natural working styles and behaviour** - encourage staff to use their natural and preferred working style and behaviour as long as they are consistent with the achievement of your organisational objectives.

4. **Discourage stereotyping** - discourage staff from imposing stereotypes and styles of working which are inconsistent with individuals' backgrounds.

5. **Discourage rigid approaches** - where particular styles of working are inhibited without good work-related reasons, provide feedback and suggestions to encourage more diverse approaches.

6. **Give feedback and suggestions sensitively** - where the style of working is inhibiting achievement of objectives, give feedback and suggestions to individuals in ways which are sensitive to their racial, social, gender or physical circumstances.

7. **Challenge discriminatory behaviour** - clearly explain the problems this behaviour may cause and the sanctions which will be applied if it continues.

8. **Implement disciplinary procedures** - take prompt action where unfair discriminatory behaviour persists.

9. **Seek guidance and support** - where you are unsure of the effect of your own, a member of your staff's or a colleague's behaviour on another person, seek guidance and support from specialists, inside or outside your organisation.

Managing Finance

Managing Finance is about establishing and agreeing budgets for providing services to customers, and ensuring that costs are kept to a minimum. It involves:

Managing Budgets

This section is about making sure projects and operations meet their financial targets.

The checklists will help you to:

- prepare estimates of income and expenditure based on the best information available
- negotiate effectively with those who have to agree the budget
- regularly check on performance against budget and make modifications where appropriate.

The process for *Managing Budgets* looks like this:

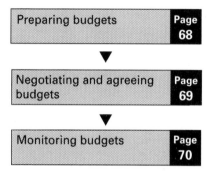

Preparing budgets	**Page 68**

▼

Negotiating and agreeing budgets	**Page 69**

▼

Monitoring budgets	**Page 70**

Preparing budgets

1. **Prepare accurate estimates of benefits, income and costs** - base your estimates on valid, reliable information, with historical data and trends where available.

2. **Assess alternative courses of action** - before submitting your budget and recommending expenditure assess the relative benefits and costs of alternative courses of action.

3. **Encourage staff to contribute to the budget** - if staff are involved in the process of drawing up the budget, they will be more committed to achieving the benefits and income and keeping within agreed costs.

4. **Clearly indicate the benefits over time** - be sure to specify what will be the net benefit from the expenditure.

5. **State your assumptions** - make it clear what assumptions you have made and why.

6. **Allow for contingencies** - take into account future changes which may affect the level of income and expenditure.

7. **Check your budgets with others** - where other people have been involved in providing information or making suggestions, check the details with them before submitting your final budget.

8. **Present your budget clearly and concisely** - make use of any forms which your organisation may have developed for presenting budgets.

9. **Be prepared to give a fuller explanation** - have all your information and arguments to hand to counter any challenges to your proposed budget.

10. **Learn from your experience** - compare actual costs and benefits with the budget and use this information to help you improve your budgeting in the future.

Negotiating and agreeing budgets

1. **Prepare people in advance** - involve your staff, colleagues and those who will be agreeing the budgets in discussing assumptions and drawing up the budgets.

2. **State your assumptions and the contingencies allowed for** - make it clear what assumptions you have made and what contingencies you have anticipated.

3. **Present your budget clearly and concisely** - emphasise the benefits making use of any forms the organisation may have developed for presenting budgets.

4. **Be as accurate as you can in your estimates** - use all the information available to support your calculations.

5. **Allow sufficient time for negotiation** - present your budget sufficiently early to allow you to provide further information if required.

6. **Negotiate with a spirit of good-will** - show that you intend to find a mutually acceptable solution.

7. **Seek clarification where there is uncertainty or disagreement** - ask for guidance and help in finding a mutually acceptable solution.

8. **Publish the budget decisions** - tell all those concerned about the outcomes of budget negotiations promptly, in order to secure their support, co-operation and confidence.

Monitoring budgets

1. **Keep expenditure within agreed limits** - be clear what your budget limits are, make sure you keep within these and check that all expenditure conforms to your organisation's policies and procedures.

2. **Phase expenditure according to a planned time-scale** - make sure you do not overspend your budget in any period, even if you are still within budget for the year, as this will be detrimental to cashflow.

3. **Check actual income and expenditure against budgets** - get accurate information on sales and costs at appropriate intervals.

4. **Report any likely over or underspend against budget** - let the appropriate people know as soon as possible of any potential variance against budget.

5. **Report any likely variance in income against budget** - let the appropriate people know as soon as possible if income is likely to be under or over budget.

6. **Give the reasons for any variances** - analyse the causes for variances in income or expenditure and propose corrective action.

7. **Take prompt corrective action** - take appropriate action where there are actual or potential significant deviations from budget.

8. **Get authority for changes in allocations between budget heads** - where you need to spend more in one budget head and less in another, obtain any necessary authorisation from the appropriate people.

9. **Get approval for changes to budgets** - where you need to change your budget during the accounting period, get appproval from the appropriate people.

Cost Control

This section is about ensuring everybody is continuously looking for ways of controlling or reducing costs.

The checklist will help you to:

* make your team aware how they can help control costs
* keep tight control on expenditure
* take prompt corrective action where expenditure looks like getting out of control.

This section links closely with *Managing Budgets* and *Managing Change*. It has just one checklist:

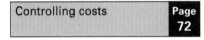

Controlling costs	Page
	72

Controlling costs

1. **Make every member of your team aware of how they can help to control costs** - get them to consider areas where costs could be reduced and bring to their attention costs they could help to reduce.

2. **Keep expenditure within agreed budgets** - know what your budget limits are and check that you keep within them.

3. **Where expenditure is outside your responsibility, refer requests promptly to the appropriate people** - many costs are the responsibility of another department; let them know promptly if you need their authorisation for expenditure.

4. **Keep records of expenditure** - keep accurate and complete records available for reference.

5. **Carefully assess information on costs and the use of resources** - regular reviews of costs will help you identify areas where these can be reduced or resources better utilised.

6. **Look for improvements** - make recommendations for efficiency improvements as quickly as possible to the appropriate people.

7. **Take prompt corrective action** - where expenditure is likely to exceed budget, report this immediately to the appropriate people and take action to minimise the effects.

Managing Information

Managing Information is about ensuring prompt access to information in order to make decisions. It involves:

Using Information

This section is about obtaining, using and presenting information to aid decision-making.

The checklists will help you to:

- identify and obtain the information you need
- record and store information in a way which makes it easy to retrieve
- evaluate the value of information
- use information to forecast future trends and developments
- present information and provide advice to others.

The process of *Using Information* looks like this:

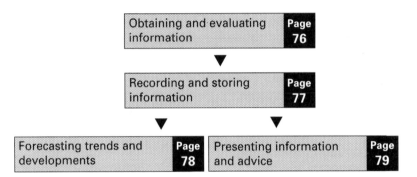

Managing Information

Obtaining and evaluating information

1. **Identify what information you require** - regularly consider the kind of information you are going to need.

2. **Review your sources of information** - regularly review a wide range of sources of information and consider how useful, reliable and cost-effective they are.

3. **Develop your networks** - establish, maintain and develop contacts with people who may be able to provide you with useful information.

4. **Seek out all relevant information** - make sure you have information on all relevant factors affecting current or potential operations.

5. **Try alternative ways of getting information** - if you are having trouble getting information from one source, try a different route in, or an alternative source.

6. **Collect information in time for it to be of use** - make sure information arrives before the deadline.

7. **Present information in a suitable form to aid decision-making** - use summaries, diagrams and recommendations to help decision-making.

8. **Draw appropriate conclusions** - make sure your conclusions are fully supported by the relevant information and reasoned argument.

9. **Review your methods of obtaining information** - review your methods on a regular basis and improve them where necessary.

Recording and storing information

1. **Record information accurately** - check the quality of records.

2. **Record information in appropriate detail** - you will need to keep a different level of detail on information, depending on how significant it is and how you anticipate using it.

3. **Record and store information using accepted formats, systems and procedures** - your organisation may have developed formal procedures and systems for storing different types of information, both paper-based and on computer.

4. **Make sure you can retrieve information promptly when required** - consider how urgently the information may be needed.

5. **Review your methods for recording and storing information** - re-evaluate your methods, systems and procedures on a regular basis to check that they are as effective and efficient as possible.

6. **Introduce new methods of recording and storing information as needed** - regularly review whether the supply of information continues to meet requirements.

7. **Analyse and correct any breakdowns in the methods of recording and storing information** - when systems do breakdown, analyse the cause, and take action to ensure similar breakdowns do not re-occur.

8. **Comply with legal requirements** - ensure your systems for recording, storing and providing information meet legal requirements.

Using Information

Forecasting trends and developments

1. **Base your forecasts on the best information available** - make sure you are using the best information given the constraints of time and cost.

2. **Make your forecasts of trends and developments at an appropriate time** - you will need to make some forecasts prior to planning; other developments may require forecasts to be regularly updated.

3. **Provide suitable quantitative information for decision making** - include in your forecasts sufficient quantitative information to allow you, and your colleagues, to be able to make decisions about allocating resources.

4. **State the assumptions underlying your forecasts** - clearly state your assumptions and the reasons for them.

5. **Clearly state the degree of certainty of your forecasts** - highlight those areas which are most at risk or where there is little evidence to support your forecast.

6. **Clearly illustrate the impact of trends and developments** - show how these trends will affect operations and the achievement of organisational objectives.

7. **Review your forecasts** - analyse the reasons for any inaccuracies in your forecasts, and use this information to improve future forecasts.

Presenting information and advice

1. **Communicate** - seize opportunities to disseminate information and advice.

2. **Make sure your information is current, relevant and accurate** - prepare carefully what you are going to say and check it with colleagues or specialists.

3. **Check that your advice is consistent with organisational policy** - check with colleagues or specialists to ensure you are providing accurate advice.

4. **Support your advice** - where appropriate, provide reasoned argument and evidence to support your advice.

5. **Think about your audience** - put yourself in your audience's position, think what information they need, and present it in a manner, and at a level and pace which is appropriate.

6. **Check that your audience has understood** - ask questions, or use feedback, to check your audience has understood the information presented.

Meetings

This section is about leading and participating in meetings to make decisions.

The checklists will help you to:

- be clear about the purpose of the meeting and make sure its objectives are achieved
- prepare and make your contributions effectively
- encourage contributions from all participants
- take decisions.

This section covers:

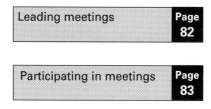

Leading meetings	Page 82

Participating in meetings	Page 83

Meetings

Leading meetings

1. **Be clear about the purpose of the meeting** - do not call a meeting if there is a better way to solve a problem or make a decision.

2. **Invite the appropriate people to attend** - only invite those people who have something to contribute or gain, but make sure you invite all the people necessary to take decisions.

3. **Allow time for preparation** - carefully prepare how you will lead the meeting and talk to other members; circulate papers in advance so everyone can be well prepared.

4. **Clearly state the purpose of the meeting at the outset** - check that all attendees share the same purpose.

5. **Allocate sufficient time** - set a fixed time for the meeting to begin and end and allocate time appropriately for each item under discussion.

6. **Encourage all attendees to contribute** - use questioning skills and individual encouragement to ensure all views are represented.

7. **Discourage unhelpful comments and digressions** - be firm, but sensitive, in asking attendees to keep to the purpose of the meeting.

8. **Summarise** - summarise the discussion at appropriate times and allocate action points at the end of each item.

9. **Take decisions** - make sure that decisions are within the meeting's authority, that they are accurately recorded and promptly communicated to those who need to know.

10. **Evaluate the meeting** - allow time at the end of the meeting to evaluate whether the purpose of the meeting has been effectively achieved.

Participating in meetings

1. **Prepare carefully** - get any papers or information in advance, and consult with others whom you are representing, so you can prepare how best to contribute to the meeting.

2. **Contribute effectively** - present your contributions clearly, accurately and at the appropriate time.

3. **Help to solve problems** - think about how you can help identify, clarify and come up with solutions to problems and help the meeting arrive at a valid decision.

4. **Keep to the point** - remember what the purpose of the meeting is and do not digress.

5. **Acknowledge the contributions and viewpoints of others** - acknowledge others' contributions and discuss these constructively, even if you disagree with them.

6. **Represent your group effectively** - if you are at the meeting as the representative of your organisation, department or team, make sure you fully represent their views, not just your own.

Strategic Management

What is Strategic Management?

Senior managers need to be excellent operational managers, but they also need to have the skills to develop and implement strategies to further their organisation's mission. Strategic management is about charting the direction for the organisation and ensuring it stays on course towards its goals.

Members of the organisation's board or governing body, and those reporting to them, will devote much of their time to strategic management, as well as fulfilling their functional or operational role. Depending on the size or structure of the organisation, relatively junior managers may also play an important part in strategic management.

Strategic management requires a sound understanding of the environment in which your organisation is working. You must be aware of what is happening in the external environment in which you operate and seize opportunities to influence this environment in your favour. You also need an objective view of your own organisation's strengths and weaknesses. You need to provide clear leadership and a vision for your organisation, and get all parties to agree to your mission, values, policies and objectives.

From the strategic objectives are developed the programmes, projects and operating plans which are delegated to contractors and operational managers to achieve. These contractors and operational managers will need your continual guidance and support, as well as monitoring, to ensure they are achieving their objectives in a way which is consistent with your organisation's culture and values.

Strategic Management

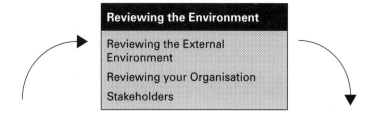

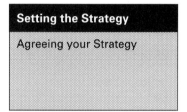

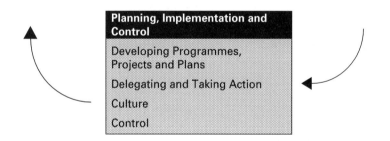

The cycle of strategic management is completed with a review of your organisation's performance, a reappraisal of its mission, policies and objectives and a search for ways of doing things better in the future. The cycle of strategic management is continuous and complex with many feedback loops and links into the operational role. The checklists on the following pages have been designed to be clear, practical guidelines for carrying out the tasks of strategic management.

Reviewing the Environment

Reviewing the Environment is about understanding your own organisation's strengths and weaknesses in the environment in which you are working so that you can develop the most effective strategy. It involves:

Strategic Management

Reviewing the External Environment

This section is about identifying the opportunities and threats in the external environment in which you operate.

The checklists will help you to:

- develop cost-effective systems for reviewing your markets
- influence and respond to the political and trading environments
- identify the strengths and weaknesses of other players, competitors and collaborators.

The process of *Reviewing the External Environment* looks like this:

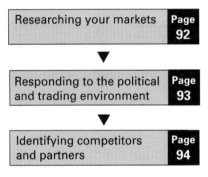

Researching your markets — Page 92

▼

Responding to the political and trading environment — Page 93

▼

Identifying competitors and partners — Page 94

Researching your markets

1. **Develop cost-effective systems for reviewing markets** - choose systems and techniques which cost-effectively identify opportunities to provide your services or products.

2. **Use field-intelligence** - get your own employees and agents to provide relevant information on customer needs.

3. **Use customer-feedback** - encourage your customers to tell you what they think about your products and services and what they will want from you in the future.

4. **Get comprehensive market analyses** - make sure the information you have on the market is up-to-date, well-evidenced and accurately reflects the current and predicted trends.

5. **Take into account possible future interests and activities** - your market review must be forward-looking, taking into account the future interests and activities of your organisation, its partners and competitors.

6. **Define your market as broadly as possible** - do not take a too narrow, traditional view of your market, but recognise the opportunities for diversity and diversification.

Responding to the political and trading environment

1. **Develop cost-effective systems for gathering information**
   - choose systems and techniques which cost-effectively identify actual or potential opportunities and threats in the political, regulatory and trading environment.

2. **Use field-intelligence** - get your own employees and agents to provide relevant information on changes in the environment.

3. **Use customer and supplier feedback** - encourage customers and suppliers to discuss with you how they see the environment changing.

4. **Get comprehensive analyses of the environment** - make sure the information you have on the environment is up-to-date, well-evidenced and accurately reflects the current and predicted trends.

5. **Take into account possible future interests and activities** - your review of the environment must be forward-looking, taking into account the future interests and activities of your organisation, its partners and competitors.

6. **Seize opportunities to change the external environment** - take opportunities to change the environment in your interest and to influence key opinion formers and decision makers.

7. **Only use ethical methods to influence the environment** - make sure the methods you and your employees use to influence the external environment are ethical, consistent with your organisation's values and sensitive to the values of stakeholders.

8. **Be clear about the constraints imposed by the external environment** - understand what the constraints are and what their implications are for your organisation.

Reviewing the Environment

Identifying competitors and partners

1. **Develop cost-effective systems for evaluating competitors and partners** - choose systems and techniques which cost-effectively identify the strengths and weaknesses of existing and potential competitors and partners.

2. **Use field-intelligence** - get your own employees and agents to provide relevant information on competitors and partners.

3. **Use customer and supplier feedback** - encourage customers and suppliers to provide you with information on the activities of competitors and partners.

4. **Evaluate the strengths and weaknesses of your competitors and partners** - make sure your evaluation is based on up-to-date information and reflects current and predicted trends.

5. **Take into account possible future interests and activities** - your review should take account of the future interests and activities of your organisation, its competitors and partners.

6. **Only use ethical methods** - make sure the methods you use to identify and evaluate competitors and partners are ethical, consistent with your organisation's values and sensitive to the values of your stakeholders.

7. **Adjust your plans** - amend your plans in the light of information on competitors and partners.

8. **Set comparative targets** - as well as your internal targets, set targets which compare your performance with your competitors.

9. **Develop the case for partnership** - where a partnership seems possible, develop a case which is well-evidenced, acceptable in terms of the risk involved and consistent with the future plans of your organisation.

Reviewing your Organisation

This section is about identifying the strengths and weaknesses of your own organisation.

The checklists will help you to:

- review the strengths and weaknesses of your products and services
- look for ways of improving your organisation's structures
- identify the strengths and weaknesses of the management team
- develop the management team
- review how you acquire and allocate financial resources.

The process of *Reviewing your Organisation* looks like this

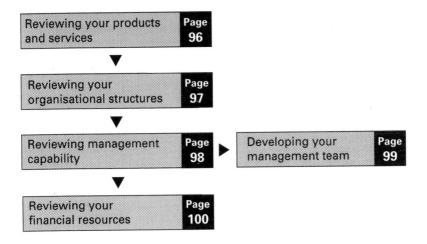

Reviewing your products and services

1. **Identify problems and opportunities for products and services** - look at both internal and external factors which may present problems or opportunities for your products and services.

2. **Use all available information** - use both quantitative and qualitative data to help identify problems and opportunities.

3. **Use employee and customer feedback** - encourage staff and customers to discuss potential problems and opportunities.

4. **Be rigorous and imaginative in your diagnosis** - get right to the cause of any problem and consider a range of other possible causes.

5. **Focus on solutions** - having diagnosed the problem accurately, look how to improve your product or service, or your organisation's operations.

6. **Search for new ideas** - use creative thinking techniques to identify opportunities to develop new products and services.

Reviewing your organisational structures

1. **Identify obstacles and opportunities in organisational structures and communication systems** - look at both the internal and external factors which may present obstacles or opportunities.

2. **Solicit suggestions from staff** - encourage all staff to suggest ways of improving structures and systems.

3. **Consult on proposed improvements** - consult with all those affected by changes to structures and systems in time for their views to be taken into account.

4. **Justify proposed improvements** - base your proposals for improvements on hard facts.

5. **Take into account the needs and expectations of stakeholders** - research stakeholders' needs and expectations and modify proposals accordingly.

6. **Implement improvements in time** - make sure you take action in sufficient time to be able to meet the new circumstances.

7. **Communicate the practical requirements** - make sure all those affected know what they are required to do to implement the improvements.

Reviewing the Environment

Reviewing management capability

1. **Identify and evaluate the strengths and weaknesses of your management team** - ensure your assessments are clear, unambiguous and fair.

2. **Choose appropriate techniques** - select identification and evaluation techniques which meet your information needs.

3. **Acknowledge the potential of managers from diverse backgrounds and experience** - develop a mix of different skills and experience in your team.

4. **Present a balanced view** - where weaknesses are identified, present these in a balanced way, also taking into account strengths and potential.

5. **Share your findings with your management team** - share your evaluation of the capability of your management team with team members, paying due regard to personal feelings and issues of confidentiality.

6. **Carry out the assessments in time** - make sure the assessments are available in time to support decisions on the structure and development of the management team.

7. **Consider the future** - when reviewing the capability of your management team, consider both current and future circumstances and needs.

Reviewing the Environment

Developing your management team

1. **Be fair in the recruitment, selection and removal of managers** - make sure your policy and practice for the recruitment, selection and removal of managers is fair, ethical, legal and consistent with your organisation's values.

2. **Share decisions on the development of the team** - involve the team in making decisions on their development, with due regard to personal feelings and issues of confidentiality.

3. **Use suggestions of team members** - team members will be more committed to the development process if they have been consulted and their suggestions used wherever possible.

4. **Consider a wide variety of development methods** - some methods may be more suited to the learning preferences of individuals in the team than others.

5. **Take advantage of diversity** - in selecting development methods, take advantage of the racial, gender and social background of the team members.

6. **Take advantage of different approaches and management styles** - in selecting development methods, take advantage of the different approaches which different managers or potential managers may take to the challenges facing your organisation.

7. **Take advantage of skills within the team** - where members of the team have the necessary skills, provide opportunities for them to share these with other team members.

8. **Choose cost-effective methods** - select those methods most likely to ensure managers are able to carry out their present and likely future roles.

9. **Build on achievement** - recognise and build on existing achievements of managers and provide feedback on how their performance is developing.

Reviewing the Environment

Reviewing your financial resources

1. **Develop systems to collect information** - you need information from those inside and outside your organisation who are responsible for acquiring and allocating financial resources.

2. **Know who your friends are** - know as much as you can about all those who can either help or hinder the process of acquiring funds.

3. **Judge your performance in context** - when selecting criteria for judging the performance of your organisation in acquiring and allocating funds, take into account the context and character of your organisation.

4. **Use commonly accepted performance measures** - use commonly accepted measures which allow you to compare the performance of your organisation with others.

5. **Make comparisons** - compare the performance of your organisation or units with other similar organisations.

6. **Look at alternative means of financing** - compare your current performance with alternative means of acquisition and allocation of financial resources over short, medium and long terms.

7. **Take contingency action** - where your review reveals threats or opportunities, identify, communicate and implement alternative, feasible courses of action.

Stakeholders

This section is about identifying your stakeholders' interests and getting them on your side.

The checklists will help you to:

- be clear about the interests of various groups of stakeholders
- develop a good relationship with your stakeholders
- secure their support and assistance.

This section covers:

| Identifying stakeholders' interests | Page 102 |

▼

| Getting the best from stakeholders | Page 103 |

Identifying stakeholders' interests

1. **Be realistic and comprehensive, when identifying stakeholders' interests** - and take account of current and likely future activities of your organisation.

2. **Use a wide range of methods to identify stakeholders' interests** - employ both quantitative and qualitative techniques.

3. **Consult widely with people throughout your organisation** - use both formal and informal methods.

4. **Use only ethical methods** - and ensure that they are sensitive to racial, social and economic diversity.

5. **Develop a relationship of trust with stakeholders** - consult with stakeholders in a way which generates their trust and leads to open expression of their interests.

6. **Take account of stakeholders' interests** - modify your plans appropriately.

7. **Take advantage of opportunities stakeholders provide** - show how stakeholders can help achieve your plans.

8. **Acknowledge and resolve differences** - where stakeholders' interests appear to be based on a misunderstanding or are at variance with your organisation's objectives, values and policies, acknowledge these differences and try to resolve them.

9. **Monitor and evaluate stakeholder reaction** - where an action is likely to excite particular or exceptional stakeholder interest, set up special monitoring and evaluation of reaction.

Reviewing the Environment

Stakeholders

Getting the best from stakeholders

1. **Evaluate your stakeholders** - evaluate stakeholders' capabilities to help or hinder the achievement of your organisation's objectives.

2. **Make your evaluation comprehensive** - consider all stakeholders and their interests in relation to current and likely future activities of your organisation.

3. **Influence your stakeholders** - encourage them to act in favour of your organisation.

4. **Communicate regularly with stakeholders** - this will maximise their support and minimise the possibility of their hindrance.

5. **Secure collaboration and support wherever possible** - ask them to make this support public.

6. **Take action to remove the possibility of stakeholders hindering your organisation** - where their interests are at variance with your organisation's objectives, discuss ways of resolving these differences.

7. **Learn from experience** - use your experience to help you manage stakeholder relationships in the future.

Reviewing the Environment

Setting the Strategy

Setting the Strategy is about consulting all interested parties to decide the future direction and goals of your organisation and enlisting their support for your strategy. It involves:

Strategic Management

Agreeing your Strategy

This section is about developing and gaining support for your organisation's mission, values, policies and objectives.

The checklists will help you to:

- consult widely with all stakeholders
- provide a vision for your organisation
- develop and agree your organisation's mission, values, policies and objectives
- gain support from your stakeholders.

The process of *Agreeing your Strategy* looks like this:

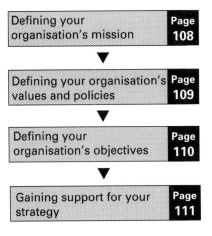

Defining your organisation's mission

1. **Consult with all stakeholders** - consult widely with all those individuals, groups and organisations (including customers, suppliers, employees and shareholders) who have an interest in the organisation to gain their views and suggestions.

2. **Describe your organisation's role and ethos** - try to capture the ethos of your organisation and its role in the environment in the mission.

3. **Make the mission both challenging and realistic** - check that the mission captures the aspirations of stakeholders and that these aspirations are achievable.

4. **Encourage creativity, innovation and justifiable risk-taking** - frame the mission in a way which encourages innovative activity.

5. **Discuss drafts of the mission with stakeholders** - explain the consequences and alternatives in order to gain their support.

6. **Reflect stakeholders' views in the mission** - make sure the mission attracts the support of the widest possible spectrum of stakeholders.

7. **Provide a vision for the future** - frame the mission within an overall vision for the position of the organisation in the future.

8. **Regularly review the mission** - up-date the mission in response to trends and opportunities.

Defining your organisation's values and policies

1. **Consult with stakeholders on the formulation of values and policies** - and incorporate their needs and ideas where possible.

2. **Be consistent** - make sure your organisation's values and policies are consistent with its vision and mission.

3. **Be realistic** - make sure your organisation's values and policies can be reflected in day-to-day work and working relationships.

4. **Include guidance on dealing with difficult situations** - particularly how to respond when under pressure or when interests or policies are in conflict.

5. **Be clear yet flexible** - make sure your values and policies are unambiguous yet allow people to respond and adhere to them in different ways.

6. **Be comprehensive** - make sure your values and policies cover all aspects of your organisation's operations, its employees, representatives, suppliers and customers.

7. **Keep up-to-date** - check regularly to ensure your values and policies are up-to-date and allow for likely future circumstances and issues.

Setting the Strategy

Defining your organisation's objectives

1. **Be consistent** - make sure your organisation's objectives are consistent with your mission and values.

2. **Deliver the mission** - make sure that your objectives are capable of delivering your organisation's mission in an acceptable timescale and at an acceptable cost.

3. **Be specific** - include sufficient detail to allow the development of specific programmes, projects and operating plans.

4. **Acknowledge constraints** - clearly acknowledge and express any constraints upon objectives.

5. **Define achievable and measurable objectives** - and state the types of measures and criteria to be used.

6. **Consult with stakeholders** - hold open and realistic discussions over the objectives.

7. **Revise objectives** - to take advantage of any actual or anticipated changes in circumstances.

Setting the Strategy

Gaining support for your strategy

1. **Consult and negotiate openly** - ensure that the mission, values, policies and objectives are influenced by and consistent with the interests of stakeholders.

2. **Find the best balance of interests** - where interests of stakeholders are in conflict, find realistic and rational compromises which balance the interests and acknowledge the tensions.

3. **Enlist stakeholders' support** - present the mission, values, policies and objectives to stakeholders in such a way as to attract their support.

4. **Minimise any problems from lack of support** - where less than full support is achieved, identify the consequences and take action to minimise any problems.

5. **Maintain regular consultation** - communicate regularly to ensure support is available when needed, especially in contingencies.

Setting the Strategy

Setting the Strategy

Planning, Implementation and Control

Strategic managers need to help develop plans to realise the strategy, implement these plans through other managers or contractors and monitor the results. *Planning, Implementation and Control* involves:

Strategic Management

Developing Programmes, Projects and Plans

This section is about developing plans and securing agreement and support for them.

The checklists will help you to:

- develop and submit proposals
- evaluate and amend proposals developed by others
- provide professional advice in developing proposals
- get the necessary support and resources to implement your plans
- gain approval for your plans.

The process for *Developing Programmes, Projects and Plans* looks like this:

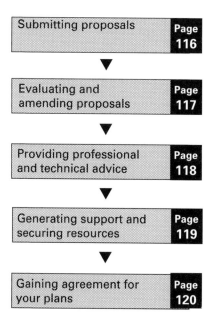

| Submitting proposals | Page 116 |

▼

| Evaluating and amending proposals | Page 117 |

▼

| Providing professional and technical advice | Page 118 |

▼

| Generating support and securing resources | Page 119 |

▼

| Gaining agreement for your plans | Page 120 |

Submitting proposals

1. **Check that your proposals are consistent** - make sure they are consistent with your organisation's objectives and goals.

2. **Consider the wider implications** - take into account other relevant programmes, projects and plans.

3. **Make your proposals comprehensive and realistic** - provide appropriate information and analyses.

4. **Draw together the range of relevant considerations** - operational, financial, legal, human resource, market and information.

5. **Present a clearly-argued rationale** - base your argument on valid information and organisational objectives.

6. **Provide sufficient information** - present proposals with sufficient information to enable the target audience to evaluate them realistically.

7. **Include measures of performance** - include in your proposals targets, standards and means of controlling their implementation.

Developing Programmes, Projects and Plans

Evaluating and amending proposals

1. **Evaluate and amend proposals presented by others** - when evaluating proposals, take account of strategic objectives and the needs of your organisation as a whole.

2. **Assess the benefits and costs** - judge proposals according to their expected benefits and costs and according to how realistic these benefits and costs appear.

3. **Check consistency** - check that proposals are consistent with your organisation's objectives, plans, values and policies.

4. **Check that the proposals take into account all relevant considerations** - operational, financial, legal, human resource, market and information.

5. **Highlight any weaknesses or inconsistencies** - list these and point them out when rejecting proposals or asking for amendments.

6. **Give reasons for rejecting proposals or referring them for amendment** - and offer help with preparing future proposals.

Providing professional or technical advice

1. **Provide advice to help others prepare programmes, projects and plans** - provide advice either when requested or when it will improve the quality of strategic decisions.

2. **Give evidence** - support your professional or technical advice with facts.

3. **Distinguish opinion from advice** - make it clear when you are offering an opinion or personal preference rather than professional or technical advice.

4. **Declare any conflict of interest** - where your own, or your department's, interests affect the advice offered.

Developing Programmes, Projects and Plans

Generating support and securing resources

1. **Generate support and secure resources for programmes, projects and plans** - communicate the benefits to those who control the resources.

2. **Make a clear, unambiguous, consistent and supportable case** - present valid information in an appropriate format.

3. **Be ethical and consistent** - ensure your activities to obtain support are ethical and consistent with the values and policies of your organisation.

4. **Recognise the interests of stakeholders** - demonstrate how these are consistent with programmes, projects and plans.

5. **Avoid undue risks** - avoid unacceptably hazardous relationships and potential damage to the good name of your organisation.

6. **Exploit alliances and trade-offs** - use partnerships and be prepared to compromise as long as this does not risk producing negative consequences for your organisation.

7. **Show commitment and drive** - reflect the commitment and drive of those who will be using the resources in the way you present your case.

Planning, Implementation and Control

Gaining agreement for your plans

1. **Negotiate with the decision-makers** - ensure their support and agreement for your plans.

2. **Satisfy all ethical, legal, value and policy requirements** - both in the way negotiations are conducted and in the way agreements are finalised.

3. **Make concessions** - but only where these are consistent with the original intentions and with the objectives of the organisation.

4. **Keep communication channels open at all times** - where agreement is not possible immediately, keep communication channels open whilst you obtain additional support, arguments or evidence.

5. **Consider the wider implications of the agreement** - consider the wider implications for your organisation and carry out any necessary consultation.

Planning, Implementation and Control

Delegating and Taking Action

This section is about ensuring suppliers and staff can deliver the outcomes of plans.

The checklists will help you to:

- negotiate contracts directly with suppliers
- delegate responsibility and authority to staff
- agree the objectives which have to be met
- provide on-going support and advice.

The process of *Delegation and Taking Action* looks like this:

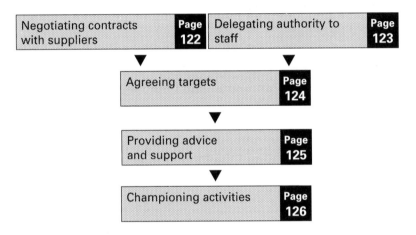

Negotiating contracts with suppliers

1. **Maintain a wide range of suppliers** - make sure you select from a sufficiently wide range of suppliers to encourage competition, diversity and innovation.

2. **Negotiate contracts and agreements** - make sure they meet your organisation's requirements.

3. **Be specific** - specify in contracts and agreements the standards, time, quantity, quality, control and consultation required.

4. **Get good value** - check that the contract provides good value when compared with other suppliers.

5. **Keep accurate records** - make sure contracts and agreements are fully documented, signed and kept available for reference.

6. **Make sure contracts and agreements are legal, ethical and conform to the values and policies of the organisation** - check with specialists if you are in doubt.

Delegating and Taking Action

Delegating authority to staff

1. **Delegate responsibility and authority to competent staff** - only delegate to those capable of doing what is asked of them.

2. **Be prepared to provide support where needed** - encourage staff to ask for support when required.

3. **Delegate explicitly** - be clear and unambiguous about what is delegated and to whom.

4. **Delegate in time** - allow sufficient time for the action to be carried out.

5. **Gain commitment** - delegate in a way which ensures understanding and inspires commitment and enthusiasm.

6. **Agree the details** - agree with those concerned the way in which the responsibilities will be carried out and the resources available.

7. **Provide sufficient resources** - make sure sufficient resources are readily available.

8. **Provide equal opportunities** - provide equal opportunities to all staff to take on responsibilities.

9. **Take advantage of diversity** - take advantage of the benefits of the diverse social, gender and racial mix of your staff in delegating authority.

10. **Review delegation** - keep delegation under review and revise as necessary.

Planning, Implementation and Control

Agreeing targets

1. **Agree clear targets** - only have targets which are necessary, unambiguous and explicit.

2. **Agree targets with those responsible** - agree and, where appropriate, amend targets with those responsible for meeting them.

3. **Take into account all relevant considerations** - when agreeing targets take into account the capabilities of the people concerned, the systems to be used and the circumstances which apply.

4. **Make your targets consistent** - check that your targets are consistent with the objectives of your organisation and the details of operating plans.

5. **Check the implications for other parts of your organisation** - where targets need to be revised, identify the implications for other parts of your organisation and communicate these to the relevant people.

6. **Gain commitment** - agree and promote targets in ways which encourage commitment to them as well as creative thinking.

Planning, Implementation and Control

Providing advice and support

1. **Provide advice and support to staff, contractors and suppliers** - help them solve problems and maintain progress.

2. **Provide advice and support at appropriate times and only when necessary** - do not interfere without good cause.

3. **Provide advice and support in ways which**:
   - confirm joint commitment to goals
   - demonstrate trust in those carrying out the work
   - give encouragement and reinforce confidence.

4. **Be sensitive** - when providing advice and support, be sensitive to the personal needs and positions of those to whom you are offering it.

5. **Enable individuals and groups to work autonomously** - only provide the advice and support necessary to allow them to make progress, then withdraw.

Championing activities

1. **Promote benefits** - promote the benefits of programmes, projects and operations to stakeholders.

2. **Identify threats** - identify threats to programmes, projects, operations and people at an early stage.

3. **Counter threats** - where you can anticipate threats, take steps to counter them in the planning and delegation of work.

4. **Consider the reasons and sources of threats** - take into account the reasons and sources of the threats in planning how to counter them.

5. **Give clear support** - make your support apparent to those under threat and keep them regularly informed about the situation.

Culture

This section is about promoting a culture which is appropriate to your organisation's mission and values.

These checklists will help you to:

- promote your organisation's values
- encourage collaboration between staff
- encourage a diversity of working styles and discourage rigid approaches.

This section covers:

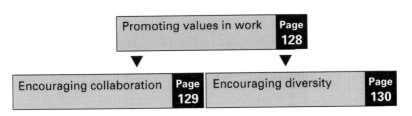

Promoting values in work

1. **Consult and provide guidance** - be clear on the ways in which your organisation's values are to be expressed in work and in working relationships.

2. **Consult with staff and other stakeholders** - consultation will help you gather ideas, suggestions and feedback on the ways in which values are expressed in work, and in working relationships, as well as gaining commitment to those values.

3. **Publish guidance on corporate values** - publish guidance to inform, explain and define the limits of acceptable practice.

4. **Use appropriate means of consultation and guidance** - the means must suit the circumstances, degree of urgency and the likely reaction of the audience.

5. **Be consistent** - make sure the means of consultation and guidance are consistent with the policies and procedures of your organisation.

6. **Commit to overcoming problems** - where problems occur which cannot be resolved in the normal way, be prepared to allocate additional resources to investigating and resolving them or to take disciplinary action where appropriate.

Encouraging collaboration

1. **Explore collaborative and consultative working arrangements** - set these up where programmes, projects and operations would benefit from them.

2. **Provide adequate resources** - provide the resources to allow collaborative and consultative working arrangements to succeed.

3. **Induct and train participants** - help participants to understand the ways of working, backgrounds and expectations of their partners.

4. **Be consistent** - ensure that targets, objectives, standards and values are consistent across the partners.

5. **Provide support** - where difficulties in collaboration and consultation occur, provide support to help partners find ways to resolve them which remain consistent with your organisation's requirements.

Planning, Implementation and Control

Encouraging diversity

1. **Encourage a diversity of working styles** - encourage teams and individuals to develop a repertoire of appropriate working styles.

2. **Support natural working styles and behaviour** - encourage teams and individuals to use their natural and preferred working style and behaviour as long as they are consistent with the achievement of your organisation's objectives.

3. **Discourage stereotyping** - discourage teams and individuals from imposing stereotypes and styles of working which are inconsistent with individuals' backgrounds.

4. **Discourage rigid approaches** - where particular styles of working are inhibited without good work-related reasons, provide feedback and suggestions to encourage more diverse approaches.

5. **Give feedback and suggestions sensitively** - where the style of working is inhibiting achievement of objectives, give feedback and suggestions to individuals in ways which are sensitive to their racial, social, gender or physical circumstances.

Planning, Implementation and Control

Control

This section is about developing a system to ensure you meet objectives and continue to improve your organisation's performance.

The checklists will help you to:

* develop appropriate indicators to measure performance
* review the performance of projects and programmes against these indicators.

The process of *Control* looks like this:

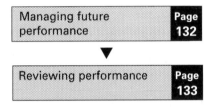

Managing future performance

1. **Propose and agree systems** - develop systems to help you manage future performance.

2. **Draw on experience** - when designing systems for managing future performance, draw on your experience of current systems and on the ideas and advice of participants and experts.

3. **Develop key indicators to control your organisation's performance** - develop key financial and other indicators to be able to monitor programmes, projects and plans.

4. **Select realistic indicators** - select indicators, and the means of measuring them which are feasible, realistic and cost-effective.

5. **Select timely indicators** - select indicators which will provide you with information in time to allow you to respond effectively.

6. **Select reliable indicators** - select indicators which provide information to help you evaluate progress and predict future outcomes with a degree of certainty sufficient for decision-making.

7. **Encourage participants to contribute** - develop systems which encourage participants to contribute to their own evaluation and allow for a diversity of contributions.

8. **Identify the support needed** - ensure that systems identify the range of support required to enable performance targets to be met.

9. **Explain systems clearly to all participants** - check their understanding and encourage them to ask for clarification.

10. **Be ethical** - make sure your systems are ethical in concept and operation.

Reviewing performance

1. **Obtain and evaluate data** - obtain and evaluate data on performance against your key indicators.

2. **Evaluate in time** - evaluate your performance at a time and frequency which allows you to control progress and make an effective response.

3. **Keep stakeholders informed** - evaluate your performance at a time and frequency which allows you to provide stakeholders with up-to-date plans.

4. **Respond to contingencies** - evaluate your performance in a way which allows you to respond rapidly to contingencies or external factors.

5. **Take differing views into account** - when evaluating your performance, take into account the views of those involved in the operations and resolve, or report, any differences of view.

6. **Report potential problems** - report any potential problems in meeting performance targets to those who need to know in time for contingency action to be taken.

7. **Be ethical** - ensure that you obtain data and evaluate it in an ethical manner.

Planning, Implementation and Control

Evaluating and Improving Performance

Evaluating and Improving Performance is about checking that your organisation is on course for achieving its goals and finding ways of improving its performance in the future. It involves:

Strategic Management

Evaluating and Improving Your Organisation's Performance

This section is about evaluating your organisation's performance in achieving its mission, objectives and policies and looking for ways to improve performance overall.

The checklists will help you to:

- develop, and evaluate your performance, against appropriate measures and criteria
- identify why you have succeeded or failed
- consult with stakeholders about the findings
- reconsider your organisation's mission, objectives and policies in the light of these findings.

The process for *Evaluating and Improving Your Organisation's Performance* looks like this:

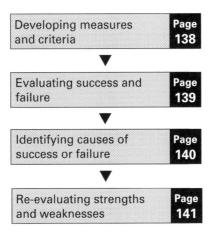

Developing measures and criteria	**Page 138**
Evaluating success and failure	**Page 139**
Identifying causes of success or failure	**Page 140**
Re-evaluating strengths and weaknesses	**Page 141**

Developing measures and criteria

1. **Develop techniques to evaluate your performance** - develop
   measures and criteria to evaluate the achievement of your
   organisation's mission, objectives and policies.

2. **Select appropriate measures and criteria** - make sure they are
   appropriate to the nature and character of your mission, objectives
   and policies.

3. **Use cost-effective measures and criteria** - make optimum use of
   existing sources of data and means of data gathering.

4. **Get timely information** - choose measures and criteria which will
   provide you with information in time for you to respond
   effectively.

5. **Get sufficient information to be able to make judgements**
   - choose measures and criteria which will give you sufficient
   information to make judgements about progress towards your
   mission and objectives and the implementation of your policies.

6. **Take into account stakeholders interests** - include the
   perspectives of your stakeholders in your measures and criteria.

Evaluating success and failure

1   **Evaluate your organisation's performance** - evaluate the extent to which your organisation's mission, objectives and policies are being achieved.

2. **Consider all the evidence** - both planned measures and informal sources of information.

3. **Provide detailed conclusions against agreed criteria** - support these conclusions with facts.

4. **Provide a rounded picture of your organisation's performance** - in respect of your mission, objectives and policies.

5. **Discuss possible reasons for failure** - where performance fails to meet the agreed criteria, suggest possible reasons and discuss these with stakeholders.

6. **Consult with stakeholders** - consult prior to the publication of any report on performance which may affect the interests of stakeholders.

7. **Be fair and ethical** - make sure your evaluation is ethical, realistic and without favour to any groups or individuals.

Evaluating and Improving Performance

Identifying causes of success or failure

1. **Look for the causes of success or failure** - find out why the objectives of programmes, projects and operating plans are, or are not, being achieved.

2. **Provide evidence** - support your explanations of the causes of success or failure with facts.

3. **Evaluate your explanations** - estimate how likely it is that these are the real causes.

4. **Explain your preferences** - where there are alternative explanations, report these and state the reason for your preference.

5. **Present your arguments logically and comprehensively** - and summarise the arguments in ways which suit different audiences.

6. **Prepare for objections** - where it is difficult to find a remedy for a cause, prepare your arguments to counter possible objections.

7. **Learn from experience** - draw the lessons from success or failure and make these available to those who could learn from them, and use them in your future planning.

8. **Provide feedback to those whose performance is examined** - clearly explain the causes identified and encourage them to use this information to improve future performance.

Re-evaluating strengths and weaknesses

1. **Re-evaluate your organisation** - consider the strengths and weaknesses of your organisation's mission, objectives and policies.

2. **Re-consider evaluations of performance and achievement.**

3. **Re-consider stakeholders interests and views.**

4. **Re-consider your organisation's vision and values.**

5. **Re-consider trends in the external environment.**

6. **Re-consider strengths and weaknesses in your internal assets.**

7. **Provide a realistic and comprehensive analysis** - supported by evidence and arguments.

8. **Make available your comments, analysis and recommendations** - so that these can be used for the review and reformulation of your mission, objectives and policies.

Evaluating and Improving Performance

National Standards

What are National Standards?

National standards of performance, or 'occupational standards', have been developed for virtually all jobs in the UK today. The standards describe what people are expected to do in their jobs, and how they are expected to do them. There are, for example, occupational standards for retail staff, for cooks, care workers, administrative staff, construction workers and those in manufacturing and engineering industries.

The Management Standards, developed by the Management Charter Initiative (MCI), describe the standards of performance expected of managers and supervisors in their job roles. They also describe the knowledge base which managers need to be able to perform effectively. The Management Standards apply to all managers and supervisors, regardless of the sector in which they are working. Whilst the context may be different, the process of, say, counselling staff, budgeting or implementing a change programme will be similar in all industries.

The Management Standards are available at four different levels:

Standards	Qualification
Senior Management Standards (draft)	
Middle Management Standards	NVQ/SVQ Level 5
First line Management Standards	NVQ/SVQ Level 4
Supervisory Management Standards	NVQ/SVQ Level 3

The Management Standards, like all occupational standards, have been developed for assessment purposes, particularly assessment leading to National Vocational Qualifications (NVQs) or Scottish Vocational Qualifications (SVQs). However, many organisations and their managers use them for a wide range of purposes, including recruitment and selection, training needs analysis, design of training programmes, performance review and appraisal, succession planning and promotion criteria. Organisations are now beginning to link them to quality initiatives such as BS 5750, Total Quality Management and Investors in People.

The section in this guide on *Strategic Management* is based largely on the Senior Management Standards (see p150-1). The section on *Operational Management* is based mainly on the Middle Management Standards (see p148-9) and on other appropriate standards, such as those developed by the Customer Service Lead Body or the Training and Development Lead Body (see addresses on page 160).

The checklists for *Operational Management* are relevant to all levels of management, although supervisors and first line managers may find they contribute to, rather than have full responsibility for, an activity. The links between the checklists and the different levels of the Management Standards are shown on pages 152-4.

National Vocational Qualifications

National Vocational Qualifications (NVQs), and Scottish Vocational Qualifications (SVQs), are certificates of employees' competence in their job roles. They are available to anyone who can prove that they are competent in all the units of the appropriate set of occupational standards.

There are five levels in the NVQ framework. Retail staff, for instance, can gain NVQs in retailing at level 1-4, carpenters at level 2 or 3 and telesales staff at level 2.

The NVQ Framework

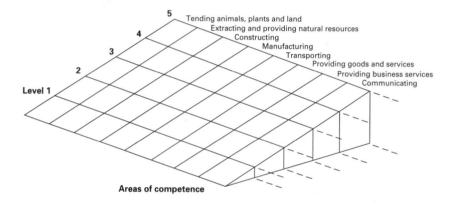

Regardless of the sector of the economy you are working in, you can be awarded an NVQ or SVQ at level 3, 4 or 5 in management, if you can satisfy an assessor that you are competent in all units of the Management Standards at the appropriate level.

You will usually need to compile a portfolio of evidence supporting your claim to competence and submit this to an assessor at an Approved Centre. An NVQ or SVQ is not a training programme. It is a certificate of your competence to do your job as a manager. Of course, you may need some training or development to attain that level of competence.

If you are interested in gaining an NVQ or SVQ, contact your local Approved Centre, details are available from the Management Charter Initiative (address on page 160).

The NVQ process

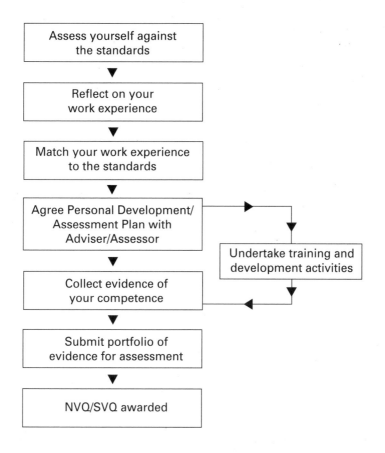

Assess yourself against the standards

▼

Reflect on your work experience

▼

Match your work experience to the standards

▼

Agree Personal Development/ Assessment Plan with Adviser/Assessor

▼

Undertake training and development activities

Collect evidence of your competence

▼

Submit portfolio of evidence for assessment

▼

NVQ/SVQ awarded

Middle Management Standards

The Middle Management Standards define the standard of performance required of operational managers with a broad range of responsibility. They form the basis of the checklists for *Operational Management.*

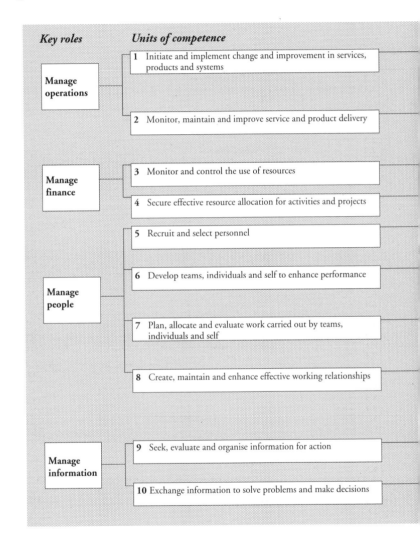

Key roles	Units of competence
Manage operations	**1** Initiate and implement change and improvement in services, products and systems
	2 Monitor, maintain and improve service and product delivery
Manage finance	**3** Monitor and control the use of resources
	4 Secure effective resource allocation for activities and projects
Manage people	**5** Recruit and select personnel
	6 Develop teams, individuals and self to enhance performance
	7 Plan, allocate and evaluate work carried out by teams, individuals and self
	8 Create, maintain and enhance effective working relationships
Manage information	**9** Seek, evaluate and organise information for action
	10 Exchange information to solve problems and make decisions

Elements of competence

1.1	Identify opportunities for improvement in services, products and systems
1.2	Evaluate proposed changes for benefits and disadvantages
1.3	Negotiate and agree the introduction of change
1.4	Implement and evaluate changes to services, products and systems
1.5	Introduce, develop and evaluate quality assurance systems

2.1	Establish and maintain the supply of resources into the organisation/department
2.2	Establish and agree customer requirements
2.3	Maintain and improve operations against quality and functional specifications
2.4	Create and maintain the necessary conditions for productive work activity

3.1	Control costs and enhance value
3.2	Monitor and control activities against budgets

4.1	Justify proposals for expenditure on projects
4.2	Negotiate and agree budgets

5.1	Define future personnel requirements
5.2	Determine specifications to secure quality people
5.3	Assess and select candidates against team and organisational requirements

6.1	Develop and improve teams through planning and activities
6.2	Identify, review and improve development activities for individuals
6.3	Develop oneself within the job role
6.4	Evaluate and improve the development processes used

7.1	Set and update work objectives for teams and individuals
7.2	Plan activities and determine work methods to achieve objectives
7.3	Allocate work and evaluate teams, individuals and self against objectives
7.4	Provide feedback to teams and individuals on their performance

8.1	Establish and maintain the trust and support of one's subordinates
8.2	Establish and maintain the trust and support of one's immediate manager
8.3	Establish and maintain relationships with colleagues
8.4	Identify and minimise interpersonal conflict
8.5	Implement disciplinary and grievance procedures
8.6	Counsel staff

9.1	Obtain and evaluate information to aid decision making
9.2	Forecast trends and developments which affect objectives
9.3	Record and store information

10.1	Lead meetings and group discussions to solve problems and make decisions
10.2	Contribute to discussions to solve problems and make decisions
10.3	Advise and inform others

Senior Management Standards

The *draft* Senior Management Standards define the standard of performance required of strategic managers. They form the basis of the checklists for *Strategic Management*.

Reading and influencing the environment

A1 External trends

A1.1 Market review
Develop systems to review markets, identify customer needs and spot opportunities for product and service development

A1.2 Climate
Evaluate and respond to political, regulatory and trading climates

A1.3 Competition and collaboration
Identify and evaluate competitors and potential collaborators

A2 Internal assets

A2.1 Product audit
Identify problems and opportunities in products and services

A2.2 Organisational structures
Review and improve the organisation's structures, systems and conditions

A2.3 Management audit
Identify and evaluate the strengths and weaknesses of the management team

A2.4 Management competence
Plan how to develop the effectiveness of the management team

A2.5 Financial resources
Develop systems to review the acquisition and allocation of financial resources

A3 Stakeholders

A3.1 Stakeholders' interests
Identify the current and likely future interests of stakeholders

A3.2 Stakeholders' impact
Evaluate and influence stakeholders' capabilities to help or hinder the achievement of the organisation's objectives

---

Evaluating and improving performance

D1 Evaluating and improving performance

D1.1 Measures and criteria
Develop measures and criteria to evaluate the achievement of the organisation's mission, objectives and policies

D1.2 Success and failure
Evaluate the extent to which the organisation's mission, objectives and policies are being achieved

D1.3 Causes
Identify causes of success and failure in goals, programmes, projects, operating plans and their implementation

D1.4 Re-evaluation
Identify possible strengths and weaknesses in the organisation's mission, objectives and policies

National Standards

Setting the strategy and gaining commitment

B1 Setting the strategy and gaining commitment

B1.1 Mission
Develop a mission to guide the organisation

B1.2 Objectives and goals
Formulate objectives and goals to carry out the mission

B1.3 Values and policies
Draw together values and policies to guide the organisation

B1.4 Gaining support
Gain support for the organisation's mission, objectives, goals, values and policies

Planning, implementation and control

C1 Programmes, projects and plans

C1.1 Submitting proposals
Submit proposals for programmes, projects and plans to meet strategic objectives and goals, and to win contracts

C1.2 Evaluating proposals
Evaluate and amend proposals in the light of strategic objectives and the needs of the organisation as a whole

C1.3 Professional advice
Provide professional and technical advice on preparing programmes, projects and operating plans

C1.4 Generating support and securing resources
Generate support and secure resources for programmes, projects and operating plans

C1.5 Securing agreement
Negotiate and secure agreement for plans

C2 Delegation and action

C2.1 Delegating authority
Delegate responsibility and authority for areas of action within the organisation

C2.2 Contracts
Negotiate contracts and agreements with internal and external providers of goods and services

C2.3 Targets
Agree targets for people and units inside and outside the organisation

C2.4 Advice
Provide advice and support to staff, contractors and suppliers to solve problems and maintain progress

C2.5 Championing
Promote and protect planned work and those who carry it out

C3 Culture

C3.1 Diversity
Encourage a diversity of working styles among teams and individuals consistent with the achievement of organisational objectives

C3.2 Collaboration
Identify and set up collaborative and consultative working arrangements

C3.3 Values in work
Consult and provide guidance on the ways in which values are to be expressed in work and working relationships

C4 Control

C4.1 Key indicators
Select key financial and other indicators to control programmes, projects and plans

C4.2 Performance review
Obtain and evaluate data on performance against key indicators and update plans and schedules

C4.3 Future performance
Propose and agree systems for managing future performance

National Standards

Links between the Checklists and the Management Standards

Operational Management Checklists	Middle Management	First Line Management	Supervisory Management
Meeting Customer Needs			
Establishing and agreeing customer requirements	2.2		
Maintaining supplies	2.1		
Maintaining a productive work environment	2.4	1.2	1.2
Meeting customer specifications	2.3	1.1	1.1
Solving problems for customers			
Managing Change			
Identifying opportunities for improvements	1.1		
Assessing the pros and cons of change	1.2	2.1	
Negotiating and agreeing the introduction of change	1.3		
Implementing and evaluating changes	1.4	2.2	
Quality Assurance			
Assuring quality	1.5		
Time Management			
Managing your time			
Personnel Planning			
Planning human resource requirements	5.1	4.1	3.1
Drawing up job specifications	5.2		
Assessing and selecting staff	5.3	4.2	3.1
Making staff redundant			
Developing Teams and Individuals			
Developing teams	6.1	5.1	4.1
Developing individuals	6.2	5.2	4.1
Developing yourself	6.3	5.3	4.4
Coaching			4.2
Mentoring			
Evaluating and improving training and development	6.4	5.2	4.3
Managing Teams and Individuals			
Planning work	7.2	6.2	5.1
Allocating work	7.3	6.3	5.2
Setting objectives	7.1	6.1	5.2
Giving feedback	7.4	6.4	5.3
Working Relationships			
Building a relationship with your manager	8.2	7.2	6.2
Building relationships with staff	8.1	7.1	6.1
Building relationships with colleagues	8.3	7.3	6.1
Minimising conflict	8.4	7.4	6.3
Managing Problems with Staff			
Counselling	8.6	7.6	
Implementing grievance and disciplinary procedures	8.5	7.5	6.4
Firing staff			

National Standards

Operational Management Checklists	Middle Management	First Line Management	Supervisory Management
Equal Opportunities			
Promoting equal opportunities			
Encouraging diversity and fair working practices			
Managing Budgets			
Preparing budgets	4.1	3.1	2.1
Negotiating and agreeing budgets	4.2		
Monitoring budgets	3.2	3.2	2.2
Cost Control			
Controlling costs	3.1	3.2	2.2
Using Information			
Obtaining and evaluating information	9.1	8.1	7.1
Recording and storing information	9.3	8.2	7.1
Forecasting trends and developments	9.2		
Presenting information and advice	10.3	9.3	7.2
Meetings			
Leading meetings	10.1	9.1	
Participating in meetings	10.2	9.2	

Continued

National Standards

Links between the Checklists and the Management Standards

Strategic Management Checklists	Senior Management
Reviewing the External Environment	
Researching your markets	A1.1
Responding to the political and trading environment	A1.2
Identifying competitors and partners	A1.3
Reviewing your Organisation	
Reviewing your products and services	A2.1
Reviewing your organisational structures	A2.2
Reviewing management capability	A2.3
Developing your management team	A2.4
Reviewing your financial resources	A2.5
Stakeholders	
Identifying stakeholders' interests	A3.1
Getting the best from stakeholders	A3.2
Agreeing your Strategy	
Defining your organisation's mission	B1.1
Defining your organisation's values and policies	B1.3
Defining your organisation's objectives	B1.2
Gaining support for your strategy	B1.4
Developing Programmes, Projects and Plans	
Submitting proposals	C1.1
Evaluating and amending proposals	C1.2
Providing professional or technical advice	C1.3
Generating support and securing resources	C1.4
Gaining agreement for your plans	C1.5
Delegating and Taking Action	
Negotiating contracts with suppliers	C2.2
Delegating authority to staff	C2.1
Agreeing targets	C2.3
Providing advice and support	C2.4
Championing activities	C2.5
Culture	
Promoting values in work	C3.3
Encouraging collaboration	C3.2
Encouraging diversity	C3.1
Control	
Managing future performance	C4.1/C4.3
Reviewing performance	C4.2
Evaluating and Improving Your Organisation's Performance	
Developing measures and criteria	D1.1
Evaluating success and failure	D1.2
Identifying causes of success or failure	D1.3
Re-evaluating strengths and weaknesses	D1.4

National Standards

Keywords Index

Useful Addresses

Customer Service Lead Body
Royal Mail
132 Newport Road
Stafford ST16 1AA
Tel: 01785 226328
Fax: 01785 225795

Management Charter Initiative
Russell Square House
10-12 Russell Square
London WC1B 5BZ
Tel: 0171 872 9000
Fax: 0171 872 9099

National Council for Vocational Qualifications
222 Euston Road
London NW1 2BZ
Tel: 0171 387 9898
Fax: 0171 387 0978

SCOTVEC
Hanover House
24 Douglas Street
Glasgow G2 7NQ
Tel: 0141 248 7900
Fax: 0141 242 2244

Training & Development Lead Body
c/o Employment OSC
2 Savoy Court
The Strand
London WC2 QEZ
Tel: 0171 240 7474
Fax: 0171 240 6264